Bringing the Depths into Focus

Bringing the Depths into Focus

Engaging Difficulties in Biblical Interpretation

T. SCOTT WOMBLE

Foreword by Leonard Sweet

WIPF & STOCK · Eugene, Oregon

BRINGING THE DEPTHS INTO FOCUS
Engaging Difficulties in Biblical Interpretation

Wipf & Stock
An Imprint of Wipf and Stock Publishers
199 W. 8th Ave., Suite 3
Eugene, OR 97401

www.wipfandstock.com

PAPERBACK ISBN: 978-1-6667-1670-2
HARDCOVER ISBN: 978-1-6667-1671-9
EBOOK ISBN: 978-1-6667-1672-6

07/22/21

For my grandchildren Elaina, Vivian, Asa, Ezra, and Jordan—
may the Word of God be a light unto your path.

Contents

Foreword by Leonard Sweet   *ix*

Acknowledgments   *xiii*

Introduction   *xv*

Chapter 1   The Problem of Words   1

Chapter 2   The Problem of Hermeneutics   12

Chapter 3   The Problem of Historical Distance   24

Chapter 4   The Problem of Missing the Forest for the Trees   39

Chapter 5   The Problem of Literalistic Reading   62

Chapter 6   The Problem of Application   79

Conclusion   113

Endnotes   115

Bibliography   125

Scripture Index   129

Foreword

CULTURE IS A LANGUAGE. Learning to read that language is what is called semiotics. We are perpetually signaling our intentions toward one another and expecting those signals to be picked up, translated, and processed. Growing up is learning to "read" that signaling. Since 90% of communication is nonverbal (facial expression, body language, energy flow, etc.) everyone needs semiotic training. That's why, in a sense, to breathe is to be a semiotician.

"Reading The Times" is not the same thing as reading The New York Times. It takes more than cable news or The New York Times to hear "what the Spirit is saying to the churches" (Rev 2:29). In fact, in some ways these rolling news feeds and noisy notifications are hindrances more than helps. It takes prayer, study, discipline, silence, praise, and worship to connect the "red-skiy" to the "blue-heaven." A biblical semiotics mandates a pneumatological hermeneutics. The Spirit teaches us how to "read" the signs. As Scott Womble seamlessly and subtly weaves throughout this book, a Jesus semiotics requires a Spirit hermeneutics.

Jesus answered hermeneutic questions with semiotic stories. For example, when quizzed about how his followers should handle Caesar, especially the payment of taxes, Jesus answered the question with a question. "What's in your pocket?" They pulled out a coin. "What image is on that coin?" "Caesar's image," they replied. "Bingo," Jesus said, or something like that. "Give to Caesar what's Caesar's and give to God what's God's." In other words, Caesar's image is on his coins, so give Caesar what's his: coinage. God's image is in you, so give God what's God's: YOU.

Or take the disciples' query to Jesus in Luke 17: "Increase our faith." Jesus, who had a nickname for each of the disciples — Rocky, Bonarges (Sons of Thunder), Didymus (My Twin), etc. — also has a nickname for them collectively: "little faiths." When they ask how they might become "big faith" disciples, Jesus responds how? No three-point plan or draught of a blueprint. He gives them a semiotic story of a mustard seed: "If you had the faith of a mustard seed, you could move a mulberry tree, or move mountains." Increase your trust in God, from little faiths to big faiths, and see the impossible happen.

Or for a showcase case-study of Jesus' use of reframing and re-signing, read Luke 10:25–37. Notice how Jesus' story of the Good Samaritan is his response to a lawyer asking a lawyerly question but with Jesus inviting him to look at the same question from another frame — to re-sign and recode his question. Our lives change, not when we read different things in the Bible but when we read the same things differently. Jesus didn't reject the past or reject the law, but re-framed re-coded, re-signed our reading of the past and refocused the lens by which we are to read the Scriptures. The same change happened to this lawyer in his exchange with Jesus.

Plants are masters of semiotics. When they are under attack, they immediately start sending signals of help and warning to neighboring foliage and fauna. They secrete hormones that trigger the release of compounds that gird up its immune system, and these hormones are invasion specific, depending on the insect. Not just on "Avatar" do plants communicate with each other . . .. They send biochemical messages via the root system, or they deploy symbiotic fungal connections in the soil. They also release chemicals in the air. These signs and signals of the "Wood Wide Web" are read by the whole forest family.

In the mountain culture where I grew up, they took seriously the "signs" of nature as described in Genesis 1:14, 16: And God said, "Let there be lights in the firmament of the heaven to divide the day from the night; and let them be for signs, and for seasons, and for days, and years . . . And God made two great lights; the greater light to rule the day, and the lesser light to rule the night: he made the stars also."

When springtime came you would wait to plant your crops until, in Appalachian phraseology, "the signs is right." A "planting by the signs" is based on the "reading" of the "signs" and "seasons: plant crops that will produce their fruits above the ground during the waxing moon (the time between a new moon and a full moon, when the moon is getting bigger), while plants that produce their crop below the ground must be planted during a waning moon (the time between a full moon and a new moon, when the moon is shrinking).

You don't get a driver's license without passing a semiotics test: a driver's test is all about reading the signs of the highway. Semiotics requires intense workouts of cerebral muscle, both right and left brain. One of the hardest things for a computer to learn is reading signs, the one piece missing so long in the development of self-driving vehicles.

Scott Womble's book is an indispensable driver's manual for better "sign-reading," both as semiotics and hermeneutics. Don't leave home without it.

LEONARD SWEET
George Fox University
Drew University
Tabor College Evangelical Seminary

Acknowledgments

MANY PEOPLE WERE WILLING to sacrifice their time so that I could bring this project to the finish line. I'd like to thank the following: Norma Baker, Penny Shadow, Jeff Miller, Kevin Vanhoozer, Jack Kuhatschek, Leonard Sweet, and my wife Lisa. Their input was indispensable and greatly appreciated.

I'd also like to thank Ron Oakes for providing me the opportunity to teach at St. Louis Christian College. Back in 2001, Ron gave me a tremendous gift that keeps giving—the assignment to teach hermeneutics. It's a course I never grow tired of teaching.

Over the years, I've had a lot of great teachers. Without their willingness to pour into students, I would never have been able to write this book. I'm forever indebted to their service. In particular, I'd like to acknowledge the contributions of Robert Kurka, William Baker, Robert Lowery, Gary Hall, and Leonard Sweet. While three of these godly men are now with the Lord, their contribution to the kingdom persists through their students.

Finally, I'd like to thank my students who have made teaching hermeneutics so enjoyable over the years. It's their eagerness to learn that stokes the fire and challenges me to keep refining my own interpretive skills.

Introduction

I LOVE TO LAUGH. In fact, I love to laugh so much that I actually try to watch a sitcom every day. I probably don't want to know how many times I've watched *Frasier*, *Wings*, *The Office*, and my personal favorite, *Seinfeld*. Besides its outlandish and very clever story lines, *Seinfeld* is well-known for its long list of great side characters. The very mention of guys like Frank Costanza, Uncle Leo, David Puddy, Kenny Bania, or Jackie Chiles gets me laughing.

Not to be lost in the shuffle are Elaine's bosses. While J. Peterman is my favorite, I was recently watching a 1994 episode that involved the eccentric Mr. Pitt. He was staring at a Magic Eye image (these were extremely popular in the 1990s). Magic Eye images (also called "autostereograms") are colorful patterned shapes that initially look to be abstract, but if you stare at them the right way you can see the encoded 3D scene. Mr. Pitt can't see the encoded picture and he's so obsessed with it that he skips a merger meeting between two companies. Instead, in typical sitcom fashion, he sends Elaine and problems ensue.

As you can guess, it's not Mr. Pitt that I really want to talk about—it's the picture. Like Mr. Pitt, my eyes betray me, as I've never been able to see what's lying behind the obvious blend of colors before my eyes; I simply can't see the 3D image. In other words, I can't see beyond what is clearly in front of me.

When studying the Bible, we're all confronted with difficulties that hinder understanding. But confusion can be overcome through study. The greater problems lie in the blind spots, the parts we don't learn to study. This book presents a look at both of these scenarios.

The thesis of this book is that we must see past what is directly in front of our eyes and bring the depths of God's Word into focus. Like a Magic Eye image, there is a depth of truth that lies beyond what one first observes. Not to be confused with allegorical interpretation, the methods here involve a training of the eyes to see things sometimes overlooked.

Each chapter tackles a specific problem that impedes the interpretive process. Chapter 1 addresses the need for us to both *hear and see the text*. As Christians, we've been so overly trained to think about words that we fail to value the disciplines of both hearing and seeing the text.

Chapter 2 discusses the need to *recognize, study, and utilize the images in the text*, something not emphasized enough in the typical approach to hermeneutics. After all, the majority of the hermeneutical process involves word analyzation and neglects the study of imagery. This process fails the future preacher who will prepare word-driven sermons that few will ever remember. By contrast, images get into long-term memory and can be re-called more easily. I propose to more fully incorporate semiotics into the hermeneutical process.

Chapter 3 explains how we must *understand what's going on behind the text*. Due to the problem of historical distance, we must study the historical, cultural, and geographical backgrounds (settings). While many are familiar with this discipline, if we truly want to see behind the text, we must remember how vital this task is.

Chapter 4 explains the need to *see beyond the immediate text*. Over the years, I've come to believe that most debates over interpretation arise from one fundamental issue—some only see the trees in front of them, while others realize there is a forest. To help readers see the forest, I discuss "layers of context" and provide an in-depth case study.

In Chapter 5 I address the need to *recognize the literary form of the text*. Unfortunately, many read every book in the Bible in the same way without regard to the literary form (genre). In everyday life, however, we know to read a letter differently than a poem or a legal document. Not giving the same consideration to the genre of a biblical passage often proves disastrous and leads the reader off the road of sound interpretation.

Because we must *apply the text*, application issues are covered in the final chapter. I present some serious problems that prevent sound application, briefly explore the more prominent theories on application, and end with seven suggestions.

In these six chapters, I hope to aid the reader in understanding that one cannot interpret the text well without bringing the depths into focus. We must hear the text, see the text, understand what's going on behind the text, see beyond the immediate text, recognize the literary form of the text, and apply the text to situations that are often far beyond the imagination of the authors. We must all learn to master the mystery of the Magic Eye.

Chapter 1

The Problem of Words

WHILE I WAS BORN in St. Louis, Missouri, and have spent the majority of my life here, I lived in Indianapolis, Indiana, from 1970 to 1975. It was a great time to be a sports fan in Indiana and, although I was only ages five to ten, I remember the time well.

I quickly learned what the Indianapolis 500 was. And because Al Unser won the event in both 1970 and 1971, I became a big fan of his. The Indiana Pacers were then in the old ABA and won the championship in both 1972 and 1973. Finally, Indiana University's men's basketball team was awesome in both 1975 and 1976.

The Bobby Knight led Hoosiers went undefeated in 1976, finishing with a perfect 32–0 record to win the Men's Division I National Championship. And trust me, if it were not for All-American Scott May breaking his arm late in the '75 season, they would have gone undefeated that year too.

Back then, Bob Knight had a television show (seems like it was on Saturday mornings). And, in '75, after the Hoosiers got bounced in the Elite 8 (following a perfect 31–0 start), I remember Knight being in tears on the show. I don't recall a single word he said, I only remember him crying. That's the power of an image.

Unfortunately for Knight, a lesson in imagery from a later time is even more powerful. In 2000, former player Neil Reed accused Knight of choking him during a practice just a few years earlier. Knight denied the accusation. But about a month after the story broke, a video surfaced that supported Reed's claim. Six months later, Knight was fired.

In ESPN's *30 for 30* documentary, "The Last Days of Knight," it was insightfully stated that a 2.4 second video showing Knight choking Reed was more powerful than a seventeen minute story that had aired a month earlier.

WRITTEN COMMUNICATION

The world changed in 1440, the year Johannes Gutenberg invented the printing press. Though the Chinese had developed movable type centuries beforehand, Gutenberg's innovation changed the world, as it introduced mass communication.[1] One of the earliest projects from his press was the Gutenberg Bible, an undertaking that put the Bible in the hands of the people. It would be impossible to determine exactly how many Bibles have been printed in the almost six hundred years since. The Guinness Book of World Records estimates that five billion Bibles were printed between 1815 and 1975.[2]

It's pretty clear, we're a text-driven people. Or as Christians may say, "We're a Word-driven people." We place great value in the Word of God. After all, "The B-I-B-L-E, yes that's the book for me." It's where we learn of God's historical plan for his people. It's where we encounter the Christ who loves us even to the point of death. It's where we seek God for direction and guidance.

The Bible is a book like no other; it's the book the Holy Spirit speaks through to change lives. I have read a few books twice, but not many. By contrast, I've read the Bible over and over. It never gets old and God continues to speak through the text with new insights. It's a book to be absorbed over a lifetime.

Thinking about the testimonies God's people could provide about the benefits of reading the Bible brings John 21:25[3] to mind: "And there are also many other things which Jesus did, which if they were written in detail, I suppose that even the world itself would not contain the books that would be written." Could we ever finish writing of how God's Word has impacted us?

Bible readers are implicitly taught to think about words and their meanings. As a young Christian, it was quickly impressed upon me that I needed a concordance. Soon, *Strong's Exhaustive Concordance* made its way into my library. When I would run across a word that intrigued or puzzled me, I would stop my reading and get lost in a word study (a word study that I was untrained to do properly). Getting caught up in words ultimately derailed me from reading complete passages in context. Thus, what was perceived to drive me deeper into scholarship actually drove me away from clear meaning.

Don't misunderstand me. I'm not saying that words aren't important. How they are used is significant, and what they mean is critical. But somewhere along the line, countless Christians elevated word study processes over literary context. The irony is that context ultimately clarifies word meanings.

I stress this to make a point—Christians are obsessed with written words, in particular, words written in the Bible. That can't be a bad thing, right? Well, no, it's not a bad thing. That is, unless the sole act of reading, or even the act of doing word studies, is the only thing we focus on to define how well we're interacting with the Word of God.

ORAL COMMUNICATION

The Word of God is far more encompassing than just written words on a printed page. Think about it. From Abraham, Moses, David, and Elijah, to Jesus and his disciples and to Christians for hundreds of years afterwards, biblical truth was transmitted primarily in an oral culture. In fact, the accounts in Genesis were probably all oral until Moses (or perhaps someone else) put them in writing. And when the text became available, only a select few were actually able to read it.

Today, the idea of living in an oral culture is as foreign as it gets, but that's the way it was for thousands of years. God's people didn't read the text, they heard the text. Over 40 percent of the Old Testament is narrative, and both the gospels and Acts are filled with stories. It's no coincidence that a great deal of the Bible contains narrative; a good story can always be remembered and is easily passed along.

Reading the text by yourself, where you are "hearing" the words only in your mind (internally) is not the same as hearing the text being read out loud. Just consider the following consequences of reading internally:

- You typically hear the text in your voice. Or what you hear can depend on your imagination.

- What you hear can be dependent on your reading skills.

- You often get hung up on details, slowing to read words over and over. This inspection of short phrases sometimes interferes with hearing the overall message.

- Reading internally often results in the biblical characters having diminished emotions, excitement, and inflection. This is precisely why

Jesus is most often portrayed in movies as an emotionless stoic who has never heard the words "smile" and "laugh."

But now think about what happens when you hear the text audibly:

- You hear the text in another voice and something about that tends to bring the text to life. This is especially true if you hear each character in different voices (think of the old-time radio programs that were broadcast from the 1920s to the 1950s).

- Reading skills are no longer a barrier to understanding. Of course, while public reading done poorly can also build barriers, good public reading enhances understanding.

- You only get one chance at hearing the text, so you pay closer attention and tend to get the big points.

- A good public reader can draw you into the emotion taking place in the text. The reader conveys excitement and sadness with pacing and voice inflection. Jesus suddenly becomes a real person with real emotions.

Christians need to both read and hear the text. Choosing one medium over another (regardless of which is chosen) has both pros and cons. For example, the person who always chooses to read the text tends to hear the text in one internal voice (a con). A way to address this issue is to read various translations, specifically translations of different translational theory and grade level (e.g., reading the New Living Translation, the New International Version, and the New American Standard Bible would provide wide variance). On the other hand, reading the text is of great aid to visual learners. If you can see the printed text, you can remember it (a pro).

By contrast, the person who always chooses to listen to the text may not be as prone to study the text (a con). At the same time, this person may listen daily in their car and be in the Word more often than some readers (a pro).

Years ago, I did a seemingly unspiritual thing and stopped taking my Bible to church. Why lug it around when I have over sixty translations in my iPhone? Besides the convenience factor, I made a conscious decision to start listening to the Scriptures being read at church. Why whip out my Bible, only to discover that the preacher was often using a different version than mine? And I often wonder why we feel a sense of obligation to "read" along with the preacher. Attempting to read along is sometimes trying and distracting.

I've discovered that listening to the Word is important. Good oral Bible readers will help you hear things that may escape notice when reading internally. Again, it's the pace of the reading, the voice inflection, the emotions—they all provide a different dynamic to the text.

Years ago, I preached a rather unorthodox sermon in the chapel at St. Louis Christian College. A student (Doug Junkins) and I simply got up and shared the complete Sermon on the Mount (SOM, Matthew 5–7) from memory. We each alternated large sections and made no commentary at all. We simply stated the SOM in its entirety. One student told me she felt like she had heard the SOM for the first time. Many shared similar comments. It's a lesson, in that there's something about hearing the Word that is simply different from reading it.

As a brief exercise, *please read Psalm 51:1–13 internally*. Go ahead and do it right now—and don't look ahead here before you do. When you return, I'll have a question for you and further instructions in this exercise.

Thinking about the reading you just completed, would I be right in assuming you probably read the entire text with one pace (your normal reading pace)? *Now, go back and read it again—this time out loud to yourself.*

Just reading the opening of verse 1 may have caused you to slow down. "Be gracious to me, O God" is an attention getter and as you utter those words something instinctively happens. It's as if your body automatically reacts and you slow down. As you continue reading verses 2–3 words such as "wash me," "cleanse me," "transgression," and "sin" actually have a way of changing your breathing as you grasp the seriousness of this significant event in the life of David.

Yes, hearing the text is an entirely different dynamic than simply reading it. If we want to bring the depths of the text into focus, past the written words, we must commit ourselves to also listening to the text. Read the Bible verbally to yourself, listen to the Bible (smart phone apps work well), listen intently when at church, and have family or group Bible readings. Being a good listener will prove beneficial.

VISUAL COMMUNICATION

If you want to bring the text into focus, hearing is just the beginning. Next level processing involves moving from words to images. A show called *Crossing Jordan* aired from 2001 to 2007. It starred Jill Hennessy as Dr. Jordan Cavanaugh, a crime-solving forensic pathologist.

Jordan and her dad could have just discussed the evidence like most crime show characters do, but they went a step further. They would visualize the murder together with some role-play. There's something to be learned here, as we need to work at imaging the biblical text.

Let's begin by thinking about the four examples of contrast between reading the text internally and hearing it audibly. Here's a short recap:

Reading Internally

- You typically hear the text in your voice. Or what you hear can depend on your imagination.

- What you hear can be dependent on your reading skills.

- You often get hung up on details, slowing to read words over and over.

- Reading internally often results in the biblical characters having diminished emotions, excitement, and inflection.

Listening Audibly

- You hear the text in another voice and something about that tends to bring the text to life.

- Good public reading enhances understanding.

- You only get one chance at hearing the text, so you pay closer attention.

- You are more easily drawn into the emotion taking place.

Now let's take these examples, and think about what happens when you also *visualize the text*:

- You attempt to see the text. While not exclusive to narrative, it works best with narrative (e.g., when you read about Jesus walking on the water, try to visualize the event).

- What you see will be impacted by your knowledge of historical, cultural, and geographical backgrounds (settings).

- You begin thinking about new details in the text, often details the writers do not even mention.

- You not only feel the emotion, but you begin to see it.

Leonard Sweet provides many great examples[4] of how visualizing the text pays off in helping us understand the Bible. One that stands out is visualizing the Apostle Paul being stoned (e.g., Acts 14:19; 2 Cor 11:25). What would you do if someone was throwing stones at you? You would use your hands to cover your head! Visualize Paul ending up on the ground, curling up, and covering his head with his hands.

While Paul utilized a scribe like many writers of his day, he would sometimes import his own personal writing into the final words of his letters. For example, in 1 Corinthians 16:21 he says, "This greeting is in my own hand" (see also Col 4:18; 2 Thess 3:17; Phlm 19). But of specific interest is Paul's statement to the Galatians. He says, "See with what large letters I am writing you with my own hand" (6:11).

Paul was stoned during the first missionary journey (AD 46–48) at Lystra (Acts 14:19) and Lystra is in southern Galatia. Many scholars believe Paul's letter to the Galatians was written somewhere around AD 48–49, shortly after the stoning took place.

Now just imagine the broken bones in Paul's hands, as the stoning was so severe that they dragged him out of the city, leaving him for dead. Why might Paul have written with such "large letters"? Having visualized Paul using his hands to block the stones from hitting his head just might help us understand.

It may serve us well to think about a sleuth with heightened observational skills. Perhaps you have seen the British show *Sherlock*, starring Benedict Cumberbatch as Sherlock Holmes. Or maybe you're familiar with the more comedic show *Psych,* where a guy named Shawn Spencer helps the local police department under the guise of being psychic.

Both Sherlock Holmes and Shawn Spencer have one thing in common, they see details others do not. While what they do is not a perfect analogy, the idea is important. As biblical readers and hearers, we need to also try and see implicit details that often elude us. In other words, we need to see beyond the text.

IMAGERY

My friend Gustavo Vega preached a sermon that he called *Wrecking the Roof.* Jesus is teaching in someone's home and some friends of a paralyzed man try to bring him to the event. But the crowd is so dense, they can't gain entrance. Getting creative, they open up the roof and lower him on his stretcher into the middle of the crowd, placing him right in front of Jesus (Luke 5:19).

While preaching this sermon, Gustavo tried to help the audience recreate this event in their minds, imagining the dirt falling from the ceiling onto everyone. I still remember that the chapel floor was covered with some literal dirt Gustavo threw down. Gustavo said, "Just picture Jesus with all of the dust. Sometimes it's a messy faith!" Gustavo went the extra mile and brought this story to life. He not only read the text, he tried to picture the text. It's the type of sermon that sticks with a person.

Sometimes visualizing the text is easier than at other times. Story lends itself to visualization. But narrative is not the only biblical literary form full of imagery. Consider wisdom literature.

Many proverbs are image driven. Sometimes they are straightforward like Proverbs 21:9 which says, "It is better to live in a corner of a roof, than in a house shared with a contentious woman." It's relatively simple to picture someone sneaking out of the house to climb up on the roof to get away. Uncomfortable, yes. But preferable to being inside with the contentious woman.

At other times, we read a proverb laced with metaphor. Take Proverbs 5:15–19 as an example:

> Drink water from your own cistern, and fresh water from your own well.
> Should your springs be dispersed abroad, streams of water in the streets?
> Let them be yours alone, and not for strangers with you.
> Let your fountain be blessed and rejoice in the wife of your youth.

Solomon is speaking to his son about the virtue of faithfulness versus the sinfulness of adultery. He could have used straightforward language and just said, "Don't commit adultery. You'll be blessed if you remain faithful to your wife." But instead, Solomon employs word pictures that cause his readers to reflect and connect. Song of Solomon is also image rich. Listen to Solomon speak of his bride as he says:

> Your lips, my bride, drip honey;
> Honey and milk are under your tongue,
> And the fragrance of your garments is like the fragrance of Lebanon.
> A garden locked is my sister, my bride,
> A rock garden locked, a spring sealed up,
> Your shoots are an orchard of pomegranates
> With choice fruits, henna with nard plants,
> Nard and saffron, calamus and cinnamon,
> With all the trees of frankincense,
> Myrrh and aloes, along with all the finest spices.
> You are a garden spring,
> A well of fresh water,
> And streams flowing from Lebanon. (4:10–15)

Simile is also used often in Song of Solomon. Listen to excerpts from chapter 4: "Your hair is like a flock of goats . . . Your teeth are like a flock of newly shorn ewes . . . Your lips are like a scarlet thread . . . Your neck is like the tower of David . . . Your two breasts are like two fawns."

Today, we may struggle to understand Solomon's images (why he would talk about nard plants and fawns), but that wasn't a problem for Solomon's early readers. Solomon utilizes figurative language to express what literal language alone cannot communicate. His expression is the overwhelming excitement of sexual attraction and lovemaking.

When considering imagery, Song of Solomon readily comes to mind. But not to be outdone is Revelation. Apocalyptic literature is all about imagery (symbols, visions, metaphors). We get very vivid pictures like that of the "great red dragon having seven heads and ten horns."[5]

One may be inclined to think visualizing the text does not work with New Testament letters, but that is not entirely true. The writers often speak in metaphors. Paul's infamous "thorn in the flesh" isn't a literal thorn (2 Cor 12:7). And Jesus didn't literally nail our sins to a cross (Col 2:14).

While imagery in letters is not always prevalent, it is nevertheless present. Consider how powerful the image of "shipwrecked faith" is in 1 Timothy 1:19. Hymenaeus and Alexander's Christian journey is described as a voyage, but somewhere along the way they are said to have suffered shipwreck. Perhaps it was the storms of life that unsettled them, or the impatience of not reaching their targeted destination quickly enough. Regardless, the message is that they were once on a voyage but encountered disaster along the way. And we are left with a sad picture of their ship shattered on the shore.

Hebrews 5:12–14 also presents strong metaphors. It says, "For though by this time you ought to be teachers, you have need again for someone to teach you the elementary principles of the oracles of God, and you have come to need milk and not solid food. For everyone who partakes only of milk is not accustomed to the word of righteousness, for he is an infant. But solid food is for the mature, who because of practice have their senses trained to discern good and evil." While the author tells us what he means by milk vs. solid food (infant vs. mature), he really didn't need to. We got his point!

Visualizing the text can entail recreating an event (like Gustavo's *Wrecking the Roof* sermon), where giving consideration to unspoken details helps you see the depth of the text. But I would add that many readers need to see beyond the text in a more straightforward manner. We often do not take time to process images that are plainly stated in the text. How often have we read things like the passage of the shipwrecked faith and not actually taken a moment to picture the travesty of battered wreckage?

Or take a story like Jesus calming the Sea of Galilee (Mark 4:35–41). Jesus and the disciples are in a boat and a fierce wind causes the waves to break over the boat, filling it up. The boys start panicking and think they're going to die. They then awaken Jesus and he commands the wind to be still. Crisis evaded.

It's not lost by readers that Jesus was sleeping through an event that made the disciples fear for their lives. But what is probably overlooked is the "cushion" (v. 38). Jesus was asleep on the cushion in the stern. We may overlook this subtle detail hiding in plain sight, but it speaks volumes.

The cushion is an image of comfort and peace. Picture it. It's like a commercial for a new bed where you always see these adults at perfect peace on their new mattress. You get all curled up and comfy, and everything in the world is just fine.[6]

Jesus is asleep on the cushion. There's a threatening storm but Jesus knows everything is under control. He should know, because as the song says, "He's got the whole world in his hands."

When we take time to process the things the writer has intentionally laid out for us, we find new ways to apply the message. New storms are kicking up but take heart, Jesus goes with you. It may get difficult, scary and even cause panic. But all you need to do is find the cushion in the midst of the chaos.

Jesus knows all about the cushion. And, of course, metaphorically, Jesus is our cushion. So, look to your lord and be at peace. Jesus said, "Why are you afraid?" (v. 40).

Lately I've been playing a game on my iPhone where you find hidden objects. In these games, for example, a spoon may be hidden in a bush. These remind me of the *Highlights* magazine I used to see at the doctor's office when I was a child (yes, the magazine is still in production).

It occurred to me that "finding" the cushion in the story is somewhat similar to finding these hidden objects. After we read the biblical account, we should consider going back and re-reading it again slowly and thoughtfully. Often, it's only after we process the obvious items that we are able to see the spoon in the bush. To bring the depths of the text into focus, patience must be practiced.

FINAL THOUGHTS

While most of us probably read the Bible, we must move from solely reading the text to also listening and seeing the text. In the end, we want to try and understand what's written with an array of senses. When Jesus talks about the lilies in the field (Matt 6:28), can you see the picture?

My wife Lisa loves lilies, in particular, Easter lilies. She loves how they look. She says, "They look like megaphones announcing the good news. Their white color adds a freshness that proclaims new life." She also thinks their fragrance is lovely. Can you see them, smell them?

Imagine how a simple bouquet of lilies brightens the smile of my wife. Now picture a field of lilies. This is the beauty Jesus describes, a beauty that God creates and maintains. If he can care for the lilies, surely, he will care for us!

To see beyond the text, we must listen and look closely at the details that often escape our mind's eye. We have to see what people typically don't focus on or fail to see at all.

Being a sports addict who lives in St. Louis, Missouri, I love both the St. Louis Blues and St. Louis Cardinals. The Cardinals had a pitcher named Chris Carpenter (2005 N.L. Cy Young award winner) who had a knack for seeing opposing pitchers tip their pitches.

On particular days when he wasn't pitching, he'd sit in the dugout and study pitcher's habits. For example, a pitcher might, for some odd reason, touch his ear every time before he throws a curveball. Once someone like Carpenter figures this out and relays it to his teammates, they can easily sit on the curveball and wreak havoc on the opposing pitcher.

Reflecting on Carpenter's ability to see pitchers tip their pitches, spoke to me about the patience and dedication it took to see what nobody else in the ballpark was seeing. And it's that patience and dedication that inspires me to look closer at the biblical text. Let's aspire to see everything in the text that the Holy Spirit would reveal.

Chapter 2

The Problem of Hermeneutics

I GAVE MY LIFE to Christ when I was nineteen years old. A short time later, I began working third shift at a bank in downtown St. Louis. Mondays were brutally busy and, at times, I literally had to run to meet deadlines with the Federal Reserve Bank of St. Louis. A break on Monday night was about as likely as winning the lottery.

But with each passing day of the week, the workload was less and less. Unless it was the end of the month or time for folks to cash their Social Security checks, Thursdays and Fridays were often the antitheses of Monday. On those nights I found myself with lots of dead time. This provided a great opportunity to read God's Word without much distraction.

My love for God's Word grew tremendously during those long, and sometimes lonely, nights. While having absolutely no training in how to interpret the Bible, I was at least able to get familiar with Old Testament narrative, which was awesome. Having not grown up in church, many of the Bible stories were new to me.

At the time, I was attending a church that did some "creative interpretation." I still remember sitting in church one Sunday morning reading the text the preacher was discussing and saying to myself, "Where is he getting this stuff? Am I really so stupid that I can't read and understand anything? Or is this so deep and spiritual that it's simply beyond my grasp?"

Soon after, I enrolled in a hermeneutics (biblical interpretation) course at St. Louis Christian College and the light came on. To this day, I feel a tremendous amount of gratitude towards my professor, Dr. Robert Kurka. That class changed my life. I realized things like literary context, literary

forms (genre), and backgrounds (historical, cultural, geographical, authorship) were key to clear understanding. After finishing seminary a few years
later, I began teaching hermeneutics at the same Bible college. It's one of my
staple courses, and I never grow tired of it.

THE PROBLEM BEGINS IN HERMENEUTICS

Having just explained my love for hermeneutics, it probably comes as a surprise that I'm now going to reveal its flaw. Some have said that hermeneutics
is about words and to a large extent that is true. Three key steps of the ex
egetical process are: literary structure, literary context, and key words (word
studies). Additionally, those who can read the original languages will often
take time to personally translate the text. Everyone else is taught to compare
translations in an effort to spot potential differences that can impact interpretation. Awareness of the differences among ancient manuscripts (textual
variants) is also important as one "establishes the text." All of these processes
are word driven.

The classic definition given to hermeneutics is that it's the "science and
art of interpretation." All of these word focused processes help make up the
scientific side of hermeneutics.

But there is an art side to hermeneutics that is seldom discussed. Application is part of that neglected art; the lack of books devoted to application speak to that truth. The art side also consists of reflecting on imagery in
the text, things like metaphors, signs, and symbols. Due to time restrictions,
imagery often gets overlooked in hermeneutics.

Imagery demands reflection and it often takes time to absorb the
meaning. Sometimes we just tend to read too quickly, glossing over things
like metaphors without giving them much thought. But even a simple metaphor requires contemplation.

For example, in Luke 10:3 Jesus says, "Go; behold, I send you out as
lambs in the midst of wolves." We've heard lots of sermons on the behaviors
of lambs, but what do we really know about wolves? And who did the wolves
represent then, and who do they represent now?

Or take Philippians 2:16. It's here where Paul says to hold fast "the
word of life, so that in the day of Christ I will have reason to glory because I
did not run in vain or toil in vain." Paul's not talking about literally running.
Thus, we need to absorb the metaphor as Paul expresses his commitment
level in serving Christ, the amount of exertion he applies to the task. It's the
absorption of the metaphor that helps a reader bring the text into focus.

THE PROBLEM EXTENDS TO HOMILETICS

Students who attend a Bible college and/or seminary take a hermeneutics course (or several) somewhere along the way. Preaching majors follow that up by taking preaching courses. An introductory preaching course is designed to help students take the interpretive skills they learned in hermeneutics and apply them to craft expository[7] sermons.

Before I go any further, let me quickly say a few things. First, I firmly believe in expository sermons. Christians today are in dire need of learning what the Bible says and expository sermons aid in attaining that goal. While topical sermons can serve a good purpose when prepared in the hands of a responsible interpreter, I have often seen preachers butcher the Bible as they strive to make their points. And my experience is that seeker-sensitive sermons rarely deal with the biblical text in any meaningful way.

Second, I certainly do not think listeners of sermons should be able to recall everything they hear every Sunday. But in spite of our inability to remember the vast majority of what we hear, I'd like to think the Holy Spirit helps us find a nugget each week that we can apply in a meaningful way.

Having made those two disclaimers, I'd still like to offer some challenges to our current approach to homiletics (the art of preaching). Even though we can't expect people to remember every word we utter during a sermon, we can strive to make them more memorable. And the fact that expository preaching is important doesn't mean it should be the only tool at our disposal.

Can we dare preach in other ways? If a preacher spends ten hours each week (probably the minimum for most preachers) writing a sermon that is mostly forgotten, then shouldn't this tell us something? Why do we continue to fulfill the cultural definition of insanity—doing the same thing over and over and expecting a new result?

As I consider typical expository preaching courses, it's probably sufficient to say the end result is a lot of three-point sermons. Over the years, I've both preached and heard a lot of three-point sermons. Some of those sermons have been great exposition of the text. The problem, however, is that it's the exception (not the rule) when someone actually remembers even one point. To prove that thesis, just ask anyone in church the following week to provide one single point from the previous week's sermon.

It often makes no difference if the sermon was great, average, or poor. People are just not wired to remember all of those words that are preached every week. Think about it. How many times have you left church, gotten in your car and then struggled to remember the driving force of the sermon? Interestingly, though, you do to tend to remember a captivating story or funny joke you heard during the message. This can be good or bad, depending on the skill of the preacher. If the story or joke actually supports the message and doesn't just assist in grabbing momentary attention, then it's served its purpose well. But if it hasn't, we can be left to not only guess the point of the joke but also the point of the sermon altogether.

The fact that we seldom remember the primary points that were dropped into the sermon, reveals a fundamental flaw in this preaching technique. If something is not working, then it begs the question of why we continue the practice.

MOVING FROM WORDS TO IMAGES

Having studied semiotics (study of signs and symbols), I've become aware of how the brain processes images first, then words. While I'm certainly no expert on how the brain functions, there is no short supply of articles on this topic.

Between the scientific community, educators, and countless marketing firms who extol the superiority of images over words, the fact seems firmly established. "Over 80 percent of all information that is absorbed by the brain is visual in nature."[8]

Of specific interest is that while "words are processed by our short-term memory,"[9] images get stored in long-term memory. For example, "people can remember more than 2,000 pictures with at least 90% accuracy in recognition tests over a period of several days, even with short presentation times during learning. This excellent memory for pictures consistently exceeds our ability to remember words."[10] Furthermore, it's claimed that "while people only remember 10 percent of things they hear and 20 percent of what they have read, around 80 percent of people remember things they see or do."[11]

None of this comes as a surprise. Some thirty-seven years removed from high school, I can still see many images from those years. But I have little recollection of any specific conversations and I can barely quote a single line I spoke or heard in high school. Oh, I remember some "conversational moments," but quoting anything word for word becomes a sticky issue. I still talk to several of my high school buddies, and I've discovered that our recollections of what was said during events can often be very different. One thing is always certain however, we have the same images stored in our heads.

But one really doesn't have to go back decades in their memory banks to prove this. Just last week, I was visiting with one of my grandchildren.

I can still see her playing outside, but I can't remember a single word that was exchanged. One final, ultimate example is probably sufficient. Just think about how we typically remember faces but struggle to remember names.

Why do we continue to focus most of our attention on the study and preaching of words when our physiology tells us that images are more prone to be remembered? Yes, the Bible is a text so we must deal with that challenge. But our overemphasis on words actually stifles our passion and ability to process images in that text—the very images that, if pondered, would more easily move the overall message into our long-term memory.

While I'm passionate about the value in hermeneutics, it must be admitted that a course void of imagery falls short. And while I applaud expository sermons, I must again admit that sermons that fail to engage listeners with imagery seem like wasted opportunities. We can spend hours crafting word-driven sermons that will result in an approximate 10 percent retention rate (at best) or we can incorporate rich imagery that about 80 percent of the people will remember.

While we often think of the Bible as a collection of words, it is certainly more than that. It's worth repeating that over 40 percent of the Old Testament is narrative. And the New Testament contains the gospels (biographical narrative) and Acts (narrative).[12] Narrative is not to be understood as a collection of words, but rather as a compilation of stories.

Stories are not meant to be dissected. Until the nineteenth century, interpreters of parables made this mistake as they read them allegorically, with each point representing some deeper meaning. This is illustrated by some of the early church fathers.

The following is Tertullian's (AD 160–220) allegorical interpretation of the Prodigal Son (Luke 15:11–32):

Older brother = Jesus
Younger brother = Christians
Inheritance = share of the knowledge of God
Citizen in foreign country = devil
Robe = sonship Adam lost in fall
Ring = sign and seal of baptism
Fatted calf = Christ
Feast = Supper of the lord

Here is Origen's (AD 184–253) allegorical interpretation of the Good Samaritan (Luke 10:30–37):

Man going to Jericho = Adam
Jerusalem = Paradise
Jericho = this world
Robbers = hostile influences and enemies

Wounds = disobedience or sin

Priest = law

Levite = prophets

Good Samaritan = Christ

Animal = body of Christ

Inn = church

Two denarii = knowledge of the Father and the Son

Innkeeper = angels in charge of the church

Return of the Good Samaritan = second coming of Christ

Eventually Adolf Julicher (AD 1857–1938) convinced the church to read parables as stories with a single point. Although since then his method has been refined,[13] it presented a major breakthrough in interpretation. Parables must be both read and heard as story. Stories aren't meant to be analyzed word by word.

Stories are told so that you can see the events (image rich) that are being explained. And when you can see the events, you can remember the events. Thus, stories are grounded in image after image.

Jesus couldn't resist a good story. While his parables sometimes puzzled his listeners, they were very memorable. One of the reasons is because Jesus used details from everyday life that made them come to life (e.g., agriculture, commerce, etc.). He also used hyperbole (gross exaggeration) to drive his points home, which made them even more memorable (everyone remembers the camel and the eye of a needle, Matt 19:24). Parables also sometimes involve a surprising twist that is impossible to forget. Beyond that, hearing a parable makes you stop, think, and ponder. Parables are stories that stick with a person!

All good stories stick. When my kids were young, a favorite story that I told them over and over was The Gingerbread Man. A favorite with a few of my grandchildren is Goldilocks and The Three Bears. Regardless of the story I'm telling the kids, I tell it with great enthusiasm and help them see the details (e.g., Goldilocks says, "This porridge is too hot!"—and I act out a person eating something that is too hot). They get the picture and that's what should happen. By the way, think about how children simply "hear" these stories that stick, often along with viewing the pictures, but they don't read them.

When speaking to college students about narrative, I mention how a story typically has a climax (peak of intensity or conflict). A great example is found in Genesis 22:1–19, when Abraham is asked to sacrifice his son Isaac. At the story's climax, you can picture the knife being in the air (v. 10) as Abraham is about to slay his son. So, when I tell the story in class, I always raise my hand, as if I am holding the knife.

Beyond the knife, put yourself in Abraham's shoes for a moment. I picture the sadness and probable tears rolling down his face. And think about Isaac; he must have been trembling. It's in the recreation of the event that we begin to see beyond the text.

Isn't it interesting how people remember stories and images? Think about these parables that you can probably finish:

- "The sower went out to sow his seed . . ." (Luke 8:5–8)

- "A man was going down from Jerusalem . . ." (Luke 10:30–37)

- "What woman, if she has ten silver coins and loses one . . ." (Luke 15:8–10)

- "A man had two sons . . ." (Luke 15:11–32)

- "Now there was a rich man . . . and . . . Lazarus . . ." (Luke 16:19–31)

Now, think about some strong imagery from the Sermon on the Mount alone:

- "You are the light of the world . . ." (Matt 5:14–16)

- "Do not store up for yourselves treasures on earth, where moth and rust destroy . . ." (Matt 6:19–21)

- ". . . the log that is in your own eye?" (Matt 7:1–3)

- "Enter through the narrow gate . . ." (Matt 7:13–14)

- ". . . a wise man who built his house on a rock . . ." (Matt 7:24–27)

The stories, the imagery, are immediately recalled in our memory. But the same cannot always be said of "quotable" favorite texts. When we hear them, they are "knowable" but sometimes the end of the verse just hangs on the edge of our tongue.

Earlier I mentioned that I had memorized half of the Sermon on the Mount (SOM) for a tag-team sermon. One might say I know the material pretty well. But it is noteworthy that I had already memorized the full SOM many years before that for an Easter play. Yet, I had to work to re-memorize it for the second occasion. Today, I can tell how the sections of material are organized in those chapters. But I can't even come close to quoting it all anymore. Words just don't stay with me. In fact, you could give me the first, second, and even third Beatitude (Matt 5:3–5), but I still can't finish the list. By contrast, I can easily rattle off some parables, and that's without ever trying to memorize them.

INCORPORATING SEMIOTICS INTO
THE HERMENEUTICAL METHOD

Much of what is taught in hermeneutics is word driven. By contrast, semiotics is about images. Biblical interpreters can greatly benefit by taking both fields of study seriously. Thinking semiotically causes a reader to slow down and think about images. The following three suggestions prove helpful with this expanded form of interpretation.

First, identify the metaphors (and similes) in the passage. Once you begin consciously thinking about these, you'll be amazed to see how many jump off the page. This is not coincidental. "Metaphorical thinking is the way we make sense of the world."[14] Furthermore, "human thought processes are largely metaphorical."[15]

Once you identify the metaphors, begin asking questions such as these:

- What does the metaphor represent?

- What image does the metaphor set forth?

- How is the metaphor used by the author elsewhere?

- How is the metaphor used throughout the Bible?

Consider 2 Corinthians 3:1–3. Here Paul says, "Are we beginning to commend ourselves again? Or do we need, as some, letters of commendation to you or from you? You are our letter, written in our hearts, known and read by all men; being manifested that you are a letter of Christ, cared for by us, written not with ink but with the Spirit of the living God, not on tablets of stone but on tablets of human hearts."

Obviously, Paul is not literally calling any of them letters. He is essentially calling the Christians at Corinth "living letters." Notice that the image does not end there. The letter is written with the Spirit of the living God . . . on tablets of human hearts.

Let's begin by making sure we understand what Paul is saying. He is an apostle of Christ and doesn't need letters of commendation. But if he did, he boldly proclaims that the lives they live for Christ are evidence enough of his ministry and calling in Christ. Thus, they serve as living letters of commendation.

There is a lot to process. Think about the actual letters of commendation—their purpose and what may have been written in them. Now take those ideas and consider how the Christians at Corinth were living letters. We must conclude that living letters represent an endorsement of success. Thus, in spite of the many problems at Corinth, Paul's ministry was productive and there were Christians there that brought glory to God. Paul doesn't come out and plainly say that here, but contemplation of the metaphor helps us perceive the depth of the text.

Isaiah 64:8 is a familiar text that speaks volumes. It says, "But now, O lord, You are our Father, we are the clay and You our potter; and all of us are the work of Your hand." While the author expounds on the metaphors at the end of the verse, there is still much to ponder.

Potters shape the clay, and in doing so they also trim off undesirable pieces. Eventually, the potter will fire it in intense heat to bring about permanent change. The clay becomes useful and sometimes, even, a work of art.

As Isaiah says, we are the clay and God is the potter. While literal clay is at the mercy of the potter, we must voluntarily place ourselves in the lord's hands and let him have his way with us. The throwing of the clay involves a bending and stretching of it, causing excess to move upward. In applying the metaphor, we might say that as clay before our lord, we should expect a level of discomfort that is necessary as we move towards the goal of becoming something beautiful in his hands.

Second, think about the imagery you see. Images abound in the text. Take, for example, 1 Thessalonians 5. Paul blasts us with terms that should catch our attention. The more obvious images are:

- Thief in the night (vv. 2, 4)
- Labor pains upon a woman with child (v. 3)
- Darkness vs. light (vv. 4, 5)
- Night vs. day (vv. 4–5, 7–8)
- Asleep vs. awake/alert (vv. 6–7, 10)
- Drunk vs. sober (vv. 6–8)
- Breastplate of faith and love (v. 8)
- Helmet, the hope of salvation (v. 8)

There are also other words, perhaps not as obvious, that could conjure up images if we don't just skim past them:

- Destruction/wrath vs. peace and safety (vv. 3, 9)
- Christ, who died (v. 10)
- Salvation (vv. 8–9) . . . Admittedly, this is a difficult image to grasp. But as we see that Paul sets it in opposition to "wrath" (v. 9), we may try to imagine the "blessings" of eternal life.

Colossians 2:2–3 has another great example. Paul says, "For I want you to know how great a struggle I have on your behalf and for those who are at Laodicea, and for all those who have not personally seen my face, that their hearts may be encouraged, having been knit together in love, and attaining to all the wealth that comes from the full assurance of understanding, resulting in a true knowledge of God's mystery, that is, Christ himself, in whom are hidden all the treasures of wisdom and knowledge."

A friend got me interested in the show, *The Curse of Oak Island*. This addictive, frustrating, and sometimes laughable show is about the search for hidden treasure on Oak Island in Nova Scotia, Canada.

Many theories, including the Knights Templar hiding priceless religious artifacts, surround what may be buried in the fabled money pit. To date, the show has aired for eight seasons and one can only imagine the amount of money that has been spent trying to find the treasure.

It's amazing how treasure fires the imagination. It conjures up the idea of incredible wealth and the discovery of something previously unknown or lost to history. Sometimes treasure also transmits the idea of obtaining something that is so rare, nobody else has it.

Notice that Paul has surrounded "treasures" by the words, "wealth," "mystery," and "hidden." He is clearly drawing us into this image. But the treasures found in Christ are not of monetary value, and neither are they obtainable to only one lucky person. Rather, they are priceless and accessible to all who follow after Jesus.

Mark 5:1–20 tells the story of the man possessed by the legion of demons. While it's a story filled with imagery (tombs, swine rushing down a bank into the sea, etc.), there are a few things that come to the forefront. Think about the man. He lives in the tombs, chains and shackles won't keep him bound, he cuts himself with stones, and he runs around naked. Now visualize the details of these four facts:

- He lives in the tombs—so he is probably filthy, unkempt, and unbathed. Because of this he must be a frightening figure.

- Chains and shackles won't hold him—it's a decent bet that in breaking these, both his ankles and hands have taken on some deep lacerations.

- He cuts himself with stones—his entire body is a bloody mess.

- He is unclothed—everyone can see his filth, his scars, his blood, his shamelessness.

Contemplating the images enables us to bring the depths into focus. There is no mention of blood, scars, or filth. But it's all present in the story.

Furthermore, as I reflect upon the image of chains (and their purpose), it's ironic that this man who can't be held by chains is still very much in bondage—until he encounters Jesus.

Third, think about the background associated with the images. In 1 Corinthians 13:12–13 Paul says, "For now we see in a mirror dimly, but then face to face; now I know in part, but then I will know fully just as I also have been fully known. But now faith, hope, love, abide these three; but the greatest of these is love."

Because our modern mirrors[16] reflect clear representations, we probably won't understand the "dim" image unless we consider the background. Mirrors as we know them (glass) were not invented until 1835. Before that, mirrors were made from polished copper, silver, or bronze metals. Thus, Paul's knowledge of a mirror is one that provides a dim image. Paul thus illustrates how we now, while living in our earthly bodies, only know (see) in part. One day, however, we will know fully.

John relays Jesus' message to seven churches (of Asia Minor) in Revelation 2–3. To each of the churches, Jesus said that if they overcome they will receive a reward, and the rewards are always different. For example, to Ephesus, Jesus said, "To him who overcomes, I will grant to eat of the tree of life which is in the Paradise of God" (Rev 2:7). To most Bible readers, that's an understandable image that finds its history in Genesis (2:9; 3:22–24).

But why does Jesus make the following promise to the church in Philadelphia? He said, "He who overcomes, I will make him a pillar in the temple of My God" (Rev 3:12). The city suffered an earthquake in AD 17 so severe that Tiberius Caesar (AD 14–37) helped them recover by relieving them from paying taxes. Apparently, the damage was so great "that people lived in the countryside outside the city for years afterwards."[17]

A pillar is an image of strength and stability, something that would appeal to the inhabitants of Philadelphia. Just think about how pillars of the Parthenon (a temple in ancient Greece) still stand today, some 2,500 years after construction. Jesus is essentially saying, "You know how you desire stability? Live for me and you'll learn what true stability is all about."

FINAL THOUGHTS

Hermeneutics, as it is often taught, places great emphasis on words. The ensuing result for many preachers is an exposition of the text presented primarily through words (e.g., three-point sermons). The unfortunate consequence is that listeners do not retain most of what they hear. Thus, there is a need for more image-driven preaching, as the brain is able to recall both

I'm truly honored and thankful that you're taking the time to preview my book. Having taught hermeneutics for twenty years, I think it's a good supplemental book for the course. I hope it can serve your students well.

God bless,

Scott

T. Scott Womble, DMin
St. Louis Christian College
Vice President of Academics | Professor of Bible & Ministry
swomble@stlchristian.edu

Feel free to connect with me on the following:
Facebook — https://www.facebook.com/profile.php?id=100011909976004
LinkedIn — https://www.linkedin.com/in/t-scott-womble-dmin-0963a9bb/

stories and images at a much more successful rate. These changes all begin with a new hermeneutical approach.

Casual Bible readers, preachers, and scholars alike can be aided by incorporating semiotics into the interpretive process. Seasoned Bible readers often comment how the Holy Spirit helps them see and learn new things in the text all the time. Just imagine the delight one may experience when they begin processing images that were previously glossed over and went unnoticed. As we learn to think of imagery, read slowly, and create mental pictures that promote understanding, the text has an ability to come alive in a fresh and exciting way. Paying attention to these signs in the text help us bring everything into focus.

Chapter 3

The Problem of Historical Distance

Books on hermeneutics aren't exactly exciting. Thus, when Jack Kuhatschek used the movie *Back to the Future* (one of my all-time favorites) as an example of historical distance—well, let's just say I was pretty happy. After Marty McFly and his DeLorean time travel from 1985 back to 1955, the differences become immediately noticeable. Kuhatschek observes,

> The town is the same, but everything has changed. Girls wear ponytails and bobby socks and say things like, 'Isn't he a dreamboat!' Guys have oily, slicked-back hair and wear letter sweaters and baggy pants. As a car with white sidewall tires pulls into a service station, uniformed attendants rush out to fill the tank, clean the windshield and check the oil. Gas is nineteen cents a gallon, and Cokes are five cents. As we watch the movie, we are struck with how odd life used to be and how much things have changed!
>
> We also realize how many things are the same. Being a teenager is as awkward now as then. We still have school, homework, parents, friendships and first love. People still cruise down the road with their favorite music blaring from the radio. Little boys will *always* tease their sisters, and although Coke is no longer five cents, people still love to drink it. What's so different?
>
> We have a similar experience when we read the Bible. Many things seem strange or unfamiliar. People wear sandals, ride camels and live in tents. They offer animal sacrifices and consider pork 'unclean.' They worship on Saturday and work

on Sunday. When a woman can't have children, she allows her husband to marry her female servant. What a different world!

Of course, many things seem just the same. The people in the Bible struggle with temptation and have difficulty trusting God. So do we. We identify with Job's suffering, even though he lived four thousand years ago. Husbands still need to love their wives, and children still need to obey their parents. Many times we feel that the biblical writers are speaking directly to us, giving us encouragement, comfort and hope.

The strange-yet-familiar feelings we have when reading the Bible (or watching a movie about the '50s) are a result of *historical distance*. Although we have much in common with the people in the Bible, there is a two- to four-thousand-year gap between us and them. They lived in a different time, a different place, a different culture, and they spoke a different language.[18]

Historical distance is often a barrier to sound interpretation. Thus, an essential step in the hermeneutical process is studying backgrounds (settings). Historical, cultural, and geographical backgrounds are of particular importance, as is authorship. Scholars have sometimes described this study as seeing "behind" the text. But in keeping with our theme, I describe it as yet another key to bringing the depths into focus.

When we run across a text that is difficult to understand, background study will often bring light into the darkness. It is, however, important to remember there are also times we think we understand a text, and yet, do not. This illustrates the need to make analysis of biblical backgrounds a routine part of our approach to Bible study.

Because there is often overlap between historical, cultural, and geographical backgrounds, discussion can sometimes be confusing. Think about the complexity. First, culture creates history. In other words, the way we live becomes a large part of our history. Second, geography creates culture, which in turn creates history. For example, the state of Florida is warm and surrounded by water. Therefore, it attracts seniors, winter tourists, and beach goers.

The overlap sometimes makes differentiating cultural and historical backgrounds, in particular, difficult. Keeping a few key things in mind can help you navigate the fog.

HISTORICAL BACKGROUNDS

When thinking about historical settings, ask yourself a simple question, "What's the history?" Studying a passage from Ephesians can be used as an example. To think about the historical background, we would want to ask the following questions:

- What is the history of the city of Ephesus, specifically the history in the first century?

- What is the history of the church at Ephesus? How did it get started?

- What relationship (history) does Paul have with the church?

- Why does Paul feel a need to write this letter? What was the occasion/ situation?

- If your passage of study contains an Old Testament quote, ask, "What's the history behind the quote?" Then, go look it up.

Internal Backgrounds

The great thing about historical backgrounds, is that they are often found within the Bible itself. In chapter 1 we used Psalm 51 to illustrate the effects of oral reading. Now, let's go back to that passage and consider how the internal background information also impacts our understanding. Verses 1–4 say,

> 1 Be gracious to me, O God, according to Your lovingkindness;
> According to the greatness of Your compassion blot out my transgressions.
> 2 Wash me thoroughly from my iniquity
> And cleanse me from my sin.
> 3 For I know my transgressions,
> And my sin is ever before me.
> 4 Against You, You only, I have sinned
> And done what is evil in Your sight,
> So that You are justified when You speak
> And blameless when You judge.

Above verse 1 there is a critical note (a superscription). It says, "For the choir director. A Psalm of David, when Nathan the prophet came to him, after he had gone in to Bathsheba." With that note, we gain the historical background that points us backwards to quite an embarrassing account in David's life. To read the story we must go to 2 Samuel 11:1–12:15. There we see the full story of David's sin against Bathsheba, the wife of Uriah, and eventually having Uriah killed.

Once we understand the gravity of David's sin, the words of Psalm 51:1–4 take on a whole new depth of meaning. As verse 1 begins with the words, "Be gracious to me, O God, according to Your lovingkindness," you can almost sense him falling to his knees. He's ashamed but he knows how to take appropriate action; he places himself at the mercies of God.

As you continue reading the Psalm with that background information now in mind, David's repeated use of the words like "transgressions" (2x), "iniquity," "sin" (3x), and "evil" is more poignant. And the following words about God's gracious nature pop from the page: "lovingkindness" and "compassion." Understanding the actual background of this Psalm brings tangible meaning to the words and enables us to see beyond the text and into the actual life story of David. This brings the Psalm to life!

Knowing the story behind the Psalm also makes us pause at verse 4, as it now seems a bit curious. David says, "Against You, You only, I have sinned." Oh really? It's a good thing we read David's note at the top of the Psalm and then went back and read 2 Samuel. Because as I read the story, David sinned against Bathsheba, Uriah, and the entire nation of Israel (since he was the king of Israel).

Yet, David says, "Against You only." While the historical background assures me David sinned against many, he makes what we may call a theological point. Ultimately, all sin is directed towards our holy Creator. Thus, we must first be cleansed by God and then move toward forgiveness from others.

As Psalm 51 shows, knowledge of key Old Testament events is essential. For example, the Exodus is repeatedly mentioned in the Bible. One source quotes eighty-seven verses that refer to God bringing Israel out of Egypt.[19] This is critical background information, that if not understood would often leave the reader in the dark. Thankfully, all we must do is turn to the book of Exodus to read the story.

Just as the Exodus is a pivotal piece of historical background from the Old Testament, the book of Acts is a valuable resource when reading New Testament letters. For instance, before reading 1 & 2 Timothy, one should first read Acts 19. "Since Timothy was in Ephesus when Paul wrote both letters to him, it is vital to understand the historical background surrounding Ephesus."[20] Acts 19:10 tells us Paul spent two years at Ephesus, and the chapter devotes forty-one verses to his stay.

Acts 19:23–41 is of particular interest, as Artemis is repeatedly mentioned (vv. 24, 27–28, 34–35). She is described as a "great goddess . . . whom all of Asia and the world worship" (vv. 27, 37). So passionate were they about their goddess, that for two hours, the people shouted, "Great is Artemis of the Ephesians" (vv. 28, 34). Also telling are verses 35 and 36: "What man is there after all who does not know that the city of the Ephesians is guardian of the temple of the great Artemis and of the image which fell down from heaven? 'So, since these are undeniable facts' . . ."

> Due to Artemis' notoriety in antiquity, it is not surprising that the biblical historical narratives involving Ephesus also make mention of her. After all, the Temple of Artemis (called Diana by the Romans) at Ephesus was one of the Seven Wonders of the Ancient World. It was said to have been four times larger than the Parthenon in Athens and was the largest structure known in Greek society.[21]

Acts 19 supports France's statement that her "temple and its cult affected every aspect of the life of Ephesus and the character of its society, and was the focus of a fierce civic pride."[22] Therefore, "The presence of Artemis at Ephesus is vital in establishing the historical context of Paul's letter to Timothy. At the very least, she is held up as the chief authority figure of the city. This could have caused the women of Ephesus to act disrespectfully towards male authority, helping us understand Paul's instructions in 2:11–12."[23]

Given the historical context surrounding Artemis, it's not surprising to see women mentioned so often in 1 Timothy (2:9, 11–12, 14–15; 3:11; 4:3, 7; 5:6, 11, 13–15). The Ephesian women were clearly susceptible to false teaching (1 Tim 4:7; 2 Tim 3:6) and, as Keener notes, they became "vehicles for propagating false teaching."[24] This background information helps us understand why Paul emphasized that these women should learn more (or quietly receive instruction) before being allowed to teach.

While much more can certainly be said about this,[25] our point here is to establish the importance of understanding historical backgrounds. Clearly, Acts provides invaluable information that sheds light on Paul's letters to Timothy.

External Backgrounds

Unfortunately, the helpful historical backgrounds sought are not always found within the Bible itself. In such cases, we must do some research to uncover the information that will enable us to bring the text into focus.

Before proceeding, a word of caution is necessary. Sometimes, in our efforts to understand the text, we have invented history. Matthew 19:24 is the ultimate example. Here Jesus says, "Again I say to you, it is easier for a camel to go through the eye of a needle, than for a rich man to enter the kingdom of God."

It's often been propagated that there was once a narrow gate in Jerusalem, and if the camel was unloaded, it could barely manage to make its way through the gate. This explanation appeared in medieval times and is simply not true, being the invention of someone grasping to make sense of this difficult statement.[26] Jesus is employing hyperbole, a favorite figure of speech he often used.

With many resources now available to help us learn the historical background information we need to make sense of confusing texts, there is no need for this type of "creative understanding." As a case study, let's review Jesus' teaching on divorce in Matthew 19:3–10. It says,

> Some Pharisees came to Jesus, testing Him and asking, "Is it lawful for a man to divorce his wife for any reason at all?" And He answered and said, "Have you not read that He who created them from the beginning made them male and female, and said, 'For this reason a man shall leave his father and mother and be joined to his wife, and the two shall become one flesh'? "So they are no longer two, but one flesh. What therefore God has joined together, let no man separate." They said to Him, "Why then did Moses command to give her a certificate of divorce and send her away?" He said to them, "Because of your hardness of heart Moses permitted you to divorce your wives; but from the beginning it has not been this way. And I say to you, whoever divorces his wife, except for immorality, and marries another woman commits adultery." The disciples said to Him, "If the relationship of the man with his wife is like this, it is better not to marry."

This text offers some interesting study. First, because there are Old Testament quotes in the text, these biblical or "internal" historical backgrounds must be referenced. Deuteronomy 24:1–5 is the key reference, with verse 1 saying, "When a man takes a wife and marries her, and it happens that she finds no favor in his eyes because he has found some indecency in her, and he writes her a certificate of divorce . . ."

The issue at hand becomes what Moses meant by "indecency." That's where investigating the "external" historical backgrounds becomes important. Kaiser summarizes how the rabbis viewed "indecency" by saying,

> Rabbi Hillel taught that it referred to something repulsive—a physical defect, or even ruining a meal! Rabbi Akiba interpreted it even more liberally: divorce could be 'for any and every reason

(Mt 19:3), such as a man's finding another woman more attractive than his own wife.' Others have believed the phrase refers to some type of illness, for example, a skin disease.[27]

Rabbi Shammai held a much more conservative view. He allowed divorce to a man who married with the assumption that his wife was a virgin, when in fact she was not (Deut 22:13–21).[28]

Moses was not pro-divorce.[29] But he "permitted divorce for one situation—indecency, which referred to sexual immorality. Yet, in later years some of the rabbis had relaxed the intent so greatly that men could divorce their wives over virtually anything. *In an ironic twist*, this was the very thing Moses had attempted to stop."[30]

Knowledge of historical rabbinic thought helps explain the Pharisaic views surrounding divorce. While their concerns surrounded the rights of the husbands, Jesus flips the coin and implicitly speaks to the rights of women by reminding them that men are also capable of committing adultery. In other words, before you toss a woman to the curb ("send away"), you'd better think twice.

Revelation is a book most find difficult to interpret. Yet, historical background study can help us with even this most perplexing book. Lowery provides insightful background assistance by saying,

> Let's first consider the importance of the imperial cult. The Roman imperial religion was ultimately concerned with the welfare of the state, especially maintaining unity and peace in the Empire. As long as people expressed their loyalty to the superpower by participating in the imperial cult, then diverse customs and religious beliefs and practices were tolerated.
>
> The overwhelming majority of scholars agree that the Roman cult in which the Emperor was worshipped as a god is the background behind such passages as Revelation 13:1–18; 14:9–11; and 19:19–20. It was this state religion that provided the means of securing the loyalty of the people and maintaining the unity of the Empire.[31]

As Lowery points out, awareness of the imperial cult will greatly aid the reader. It's within this historical context where "Christian faith stood in clear opposition to the idolatrous claims of the state."[32]

While the study of external backgrounds is critical for understanding, they are also sometimes valuable simply because they support the biblical record and help build a person's faith in the truth of God's Word. At times, people falsely accuse Christians of believing a Bible that isn't supported elsewhere; this simply is not true.

Jesus was a historical figure, mentioned outside of the Bible. There are actually about a dozen Greco-Roman sources that refer to Jesus. They also often mention Pilate and the crucifixion.

As another example, Herod the Great is portrayed as a lunatic murderer in Matthew 2, having innocent children killed. We might ask if this is consistent with history. The answer is a resounding, "Yes." Herod not only killed two of his wives, he did the same to three of his sons, prompting Augustus Caesar to say that it was better to be Herod's pig than his son. In other words, since Herod was a Jew who didn't eat pork, it was better to be the pig! So, we see study of historical background can be beneficial on a number of levels.

CULTURAL BACKGROUNDS

To identify cultural backgrounds, the key question to remember is, "How did the people live?" As an example, if I were thinking about the things that create cultural significance specific to my city (St. Louis), I'd mention things like: Anheuser-Busch, the St. Louis Zoo (it's awesome and free), the Gateway Arch, both the St. Louis Cardinals and the St. Louis Blues, and the various foods invented in St. Louis (e.g., toasted ravioli, provel cheese/ St. Louis style pizza, gooey butter cake, bar-b-qued pork steaks, and the concrete ice cream treat).

All of these things help create a culture that is unique to St. Louis. You may also think in terms of "customs" that are important. Fair St. Louis is the annual fourth of July event in downtown St. Louis. For forty years, it has featured various free events (e.g., air shows, concerts, and, of course, fireworks). St. Louisans also love to ask new acquaintances where they went to high school; it's the ice breaker that creates solidarity.

Both religious and political backgrounds also help make up culture. In the Bible, these are crucial. Regarding the former, just think about the kings, priests, and leader groups like the Pharisees and Sadducees. The latter may draw your thoughts to groups like the various Caesars and Herods of the New Testament. Religion and politics will always be part of culture. Generally speaking, you'll also want to think of things like economics, military issues, family customs (e.g., marital and educational practices), and recreation.

When reading a biblical passage, consideration of cultural backgrounds is a must. Specifically, focus on any issues that are directly mentioned in the text.

I've always found Mark 14:12–13 amusing. It says, "On the first day of Unleavened Bread, when the Passover lamb was being sacrificed, His disciples said to Him, 'Where do You want us to go and prepare for You to eat the Passover?' And He sent two of His disciples and said to them, 'Go into the city, and a man will meet you carrying a pitcher of water; follow him.'"

I find it amusing because on the surface Jesus' statement seems absurd (by the way, being an honest reader will make you a better interpreter because it will cause you to pause and ask questions). His statement seems as silly as saying something like, "Go to the St. Louis Cardinals baseball game and meet up with the guy wearing red."

I mean, surely there will be countless people carrying water around, right? Well, there may be a lot of people carrying water, but with exception to this one man Jesus singles out, they will all be women. It was a woman's job to carry water. This is the issue beyond the text that the disciples understood.

Something interesting happens when Jesus is arrested in the garden. Peter takes his sword out and cuts off the ear of the high priest's servant. Jesus cleans up the mess and responds by saying, "Put your sword back into its place; for all those who take up the sword shall perish by the sword. Or do you think that I cannot appeal to My Father, and He will at once put at My disposal more than twelve legions of angels?" (Matt 26:52–53).

The cultural cue providing depth to this story is that this is a Roman world, a world ruled by the mighty Roman armies. A Roman legion normally had 6,000 soldiers and was a sign of strength that struck fear into the inhabitants of any enemy city that had the unfortunate displeasure of meeting one.

Here, Jesus' words conjure up this image of awesome power. With it, Jesus jolts their imagination by saying he could call "twelve legions of angels" to his aid. Thus, if he wanted, Jesus could summon 72,000 angels to his defense. This is the image which brings the text into clear focus.

For those present who knew their Old Testament, like some of the officials from the chief priests and Pharisees who were there (John 18:3), the image must have been even more startling. After all, 2 Kings 19:35 tells of one angel who killed an army of 185,000 in one day. Just for fun—if we do the math, 6,000 x 185,000 = 1,110,000,000. In other words, to those who are arresting him, Jesus is saying, "Don't, for even a single moment, think you have any real power over me!"

One of the most bizarre passages in the Bible is found in Genesis 19:1–11. We're told that two angels come to Sodom and stay at Lot's house. When the men of the city find out Lot has guests, they surround the house and call out to Lot saying, "Bring them out to us that we may have relations with them."

Lot's response seems repulsive, as he says, "Please, my brothers, do not act wickedly. Now behold, I have two daughters who have not had relations with man; please let me bring them out to you, and do to them whatever you like; only do nothing to these men inasmuch as they have come under the shelter of my roof."

This account is not only shocking, it could rock a person's faith in the Bible. I call these crazy passages "red flag moments." Being a sports fan, I probably get this mental image from watching IndyCar racing. When something happens (e.g., horrible rain) that brings the race to a stop, the red flag comes out. Stopping is essentially what happens when I read "hard sayings"[33] like this. But again, like the amusing water jar scene in Mark 14, honesty with the text is imperative, as it causes a person to dig deep for answers.

The key to Lot's strange reply is found in verse 8, "only do nothing to these men inasmuch as they have come under the shelter of my roof." In antiquity, when a person took someone into their house, it was expected that they protect their guests at all costs. Not protecting a guest would result in being shamed by the community. This concept was grounded in the "honor and shame" value system.

Citizens of the United States, and Westerners in general, are not accustomed to thinking in terms of honor and shame. This is primarily because we are very individualistic. Societies that still focus on the collective group, tend to think in terms of honor/shame.[34] If it were not for glimpses we see in things like Star Trek, the entire concept would probably be foreign to us. But if you're familiar with Star Trek, you understand how much emphasis the Klingons place on honor and shame. To bring shame to the family is the worst thing that can happen to a Klingon.

It should be noted that Lot's actions are not prescriptive behavior for us. The narrative records the event, and the cultural backgrounds help us understand Lot's behavior. But Scripture certainly does not condone everything that took place.

Getting familiar with biblical idioms is another feature of cultural background study. With idioms, the literal meaning of words doesn't convey the actual meaning. For example, someone may say to another, "You've lost your marbles." They aren't talking about literal marbles, but rather implying, "You've lost your mind." Of course, that is yet another idiom, because the person didn't literally "lose" their mind. So, a better translation of "You've lost your marbles" might be "You're not thinking soundly."

One of my favorite movies is *Tombstone*. It has a star-studded cast and with his portrayal of Doc Holliday, Val Kilmer knocks it out of the park. One of the things that brings some authenticity to the movie is their use of idioms, in this case, sayings unique to the setting of the Old West.

In one of the closing scenes, Doc Holliday and Johnny Ringo (a member of the Clanton gang of cowboys) have a one-on-one standoff. Ringo is expecting Wyatt Earp to show up, but Holliday beats Earp to the party. As Doc arrives onto the scene, Ringo says, "Well, I didn't think you had it in you."

Holliday then raises his head and says, "I'm your huckleberry," creating some shock in Ringo. It's "the scene" in the movie that fans watch over and over. But what did Doc Holliday actually mean? Well, "I'm your huckleberry" meant "I'm just the man you're looking for." Ringo, of course, is thinking, "No, you're not."

Ringo is shot by Doc Holliday. As Ringo stumbles to the ground, Doc taunts him by saying, "You're no daisy. You're no daisy at all." It's yet another idiom for saying, "You're not the best."

When you're young, you tend to know the idioms of current culture. Once you have children, however, you notice them coming home from school and saying odd things that you simply don't understand. They know the current idioms and now your age is showing! This can once again be illustrated in the movie *Back to the Future*. Marty keeps saying, "That's heavy" (meaning, "that's deep stuff"). But Doc Brown keeps misinterpreting Marty's statement, at one time asking, "Why are things so heavy in the future? Is there a problem with the earth's gravitational pull?"

Idioms change quickly, so imagine our problem in dealing with the biblical text. One text that puzzled me for years was Matthew 6:22–23. Jesus says, "The eye is the lamp of the body; so then if your eye is clear, your whole body will be full of light. But if your eye is bad, your whole body will be full of darkness. If then the light that is in you is darkness, how great is the darkness!"

Say what, Jesus? Talk about a confusing statement. Of course, the key is that we're dealing with some idioms.

If your "eyes are good" meant "you are a generous person." And If your "eyes are bad" meant "you are a stingy or greedy person."[35]

Additionally, reading the surrounding context really helps us get the point. In verses 19–21, Jesus talks about storing up treasures in heaven, not on earth. Then, in verse 24, he says we can't serve two masters (God and money). One must recognize both the idioms, and that verses 22–23 are placed within a context of money.

Once these things are understood, the entire section comes together nicely. Jesus is saying, "Serve God by being a generous person who is most interested in storing up eternal treasures."

Matthew 18:18 provides another good example. Jesus says, "Whatever you bind on earth shall have been bound in heaven, and whatever you loose on earth shall have been loosed in heaven." Many years ago, I attended a church that continually quoted this verse and interpreted "binding" to mean binding demonic spirits and "loosing" as loosing blessing on the church.

As the literary context shows, nothing could be further from the truth. In verses 15–20, Jesus is discussing how the church should deal with a sinning brother. But knowing that alone doesn't help us understand verse 18. "Binding" and "loosing" are idioms for "forbidding" and "permitting." We may still have questions as to how our actions impact heaven and other nuances of this text, but those are questions for another time. For now, suffice it to say we at least know that the binding and loosing has nothing to do with binding spirits and loosing blessings, and rather refers to the sin we need to address in our Christian community.

GEOGRAPHICAL BACKGROUNDS

While there may not be any confusion in identifying geographical backgrounds, the key question to think about is, "What place are we talking about?" Furthermore, since geographical backgrounds are about physical settings, we will have questions about topography and climate.

Geography may be one piece of background information we underestimate or deem less important. We would do well to remember, though, that geography influences culture, which in turn creates a history. And just like historical and cultural backgrounds, understanding geographical backgrounds helps us see beyond the text.

The maps found in the back of a standard Bible typically point to the most prevalent places of study. Old Testament scholars value the plotting out of the Israelites' forty-year trek through the wilderness, whereas New Testament scholars may point to tracing Jesus' steps. When reading the biblical account, we often jump from place to place without giving much thought to where we currently are in the story. Ignoring the geographical context of the biblical story is akin to telling a story set in modern day United States and failing to see how different the main character's experience would be depending on whether he was in Las Vegas, Miami, or a small farming community in the Midwest.

The seven churches in Revelation 2–3 were found throughout Asia (Rev 1:4). The area is what we actually refer to as Asia Minor (present day Turkey). Of particular interest here is the church at Laodicea (Rev 3:14–22). It has the infamous distinction of being "The Lukewarm Church."

Laodicea lacked a natural water supply, which means they had water piped in from a nearby city. Hierapolis was about six miles away and had hot springs. By contrast, Colossae had cold refreshing water and was about ten miles away. Today, we are unsure as to where Laodicea got their water but one thing is sure, it was lukewarm by the time it got to them. And as someone once said, "Hot water heals, cold water refreshes, but lukewarm water is useless." The New Testament Church would have been aware of the stark contrast between Laodicea's bland, lukewarm water in comparison to the options from neighboring cities.

Genesis 19 is probably the weirdest chapter in the Bible. Not only does it contain the story referenced earlier about the angels staying at Lot's house (Gen 19:1–11) and Lot offering his daughters to a mob wanting sex, the chapter also includes the account of Lot's wife becoming a pillar of salt (Gen 19:12–29).

To be honest here, on the surface this latter story is just embarrassing to try to explain to unbelievers. After all, it sounds like Greek mythology or some kind of fable. But if you believe in the truth of God's Word, weirdness is just a spark to spur you on to seeking the answer that is found beyond the text.

This passage is a prime example of how asking geographical questions is helpful. Where were Sodom and Gomorrah? "A precise location is not given for the city though the general area is associated with the Dead Sea. Archaeological research early in the twentieth century suggested to some that Sodom, along with other cities of the valley, is located under what is now the shallow, southern end of the Dead Sea."[36]

The Dead Sea can be described as a salty, dead body of water and is the lowest point on Earth at 430.5 meters (1,412 feet) below sea level.[37] In Genesis 14:1–3, reference is made to the kings of the valley, mentioning both Sodom and Gomorrah by name. Verse three cites the "Salt Sea," another name for the Dead Sea.

Once the Dead Sea (Salt Sea) is identified as the location of Sodom and Gomorrah, the peculiar fate of Lot's wife doesn't seem as odd. Genesis 19:24 says that "the lord rained down . . . brimstone and fire." Brimstone means "burning stone" and is another name for sulfur.

> The natural ingredients of the destruction (see 14:3, 10) were abundant in this region of petroleum, bitumen, salt and sulphur;

but its character was a judgment, not a random disaster. The overwhelming of Lot's wife as the molten materials of the explosion rained down on her is physically nothing remarkable; but in the context of judgment it captures in a single picture the fate of those who turn back.[38]

Now we can picture this horrifying event more realistically. It would appear that God created some explosions that hurled salty debris from the Dead Sea into the air, which in turn mixed with the burning sulfur. Moving too slowly and possibly lamenting the loss of her friends and her home, Lot's wife suffers a tragic fate that now doesn't seem so far from reality.

AUTHORSHIP

Upon previous examination of Psalm 51, the importance of historical background was proven. Knowing the author of the Psalm was also critical, showing the importance of authorship recognition.

Modern scholarship often calls into question traditional views of authorship, making authorship more important than ever (e.g., some today don't believe Paul wrote all thirteen letters traditionally attributed to him). The scope of this book, however, does not call for a defense of the traditional views that I hold. I merely want to provide examples of how authorship helps us bring the depths into focus.

"Rejoice" is the key word in Philippians, being used nine times ("joy" is also used seven times). One of the most familiar verses in Philippians is 4:4, which says, "Rejoice in the Lord always; again I will say, rejoice!"

Whether it's financial problems, family loss, health issues, or a seemingly endless list of items that create trials and depression, every one of us has to deal with difficulties and challenging times. And when we are in the midst of our struggles it's hard to hear someone offer pat answers like "just rejoice in the bad times." That's especially true if we feel like the person offering advice hasn't experienced the same hardships.

This particular passage becomes more meaningful to us when we think a bit about the author. Paul said the following in 2 Corinthians 11:24–28,

> Five times I received from the Jews thirty-nine lashes. Three times I was beaten with rods, once I was stoned, three times I was shipwrecked, a night and a day I have spent in the deep. I have been on frequent journeys, in dangers from rivers, dangers from robbers, dangers from my countrymen, dangers from the Gentiles, dangers in the city, dangers in the wilderness, dangers on the sea, dangers among false brethren; I have been in labor

and hardship, through many sleepless nights, in hunger and thirst, often without food, in cold and exposure. Apart from such external things, there is the daily pressure on me of concern for all the churches.

And, of course, there's a reason we call Philippians one of the "prison epistles." As Paul writes this letter, he makes mention of the fact that he is currently in prison (1:7, 13–14, 17). Understanding the background of the author removes the barrier of thinking Paul may be out of touch. If Paul can rejoice, surely we can.

FINAL THOUGHTS

Historical distance creates an obstruction to confident interpretation. Furthermore, our misconceptions can be many when we read a Middle Eastern text with Western eyes. As great as these obstacles may be, they can be overcome with diligent study. The exciting thing is that learning backgrounds brings clarity and helps the reader gain new insights. It's these kinds of breakthroughs that fire the furnace for further study.

Chapter 4

The Problem of Missing the Forest for the Trees

THERE'S AN OLD IDIOMATIC expression about the person who "can't see the forest for the trees." This describes a person who is so caught up in the small details that they can't see the big picture.

Sometimes athletes only see the trees. Take, for example, a basketball team that is trailing by three points with only four seconds to play. The point guard sees an opening to the basket and takes it in for the easy layup. While being proud of his accomplishment, his teammates become unglued because they needed three points, not two. The point guard simply failed to see the big picture.

The opposite of the point guard's actions may be illustrated in a baseball game. Let's say the home team is winning by two runs in the top of the ninth inning. The closer comes in and immediately starts challenging hitters with fastball after fastball. A casual observer may think his pitch selection is too predictable. But the pitcher knows that even if someone hits a home run, they will still maintain a one-run lead. Seeing the forest reminds him that under no circumstances, should he nibble with a hitter and allow a walk. After all, putting on one baserunner will bring the tying run to the plate.

Recently, I binged watched the show *Monk* (2002 to 2009). In the show, Adrian Monk is a former policeman who now serves as a private consultant for the San Francisco police. Like all great sleuths, Monk sees details that elude everyone else. Sometimes, however, Monk observes a crime scene and just says, "Something isn't right here."

In fact, occasionally all of the "facts of the crime" seem to point toward one suspect. But to the surprise and shock of the other policemen, Monk will intuitively insist that they have the wrong person. In saying "Something isn't right here," Monk asserts that the accepted narrative about the forest isn't correct.

See, occasionally a person can focus on all of the details of a scene, come to an airtight conclusion and still be wrong. In fact, sometimes the details of a specific scene can impede one's understanding of the big picture at hand. This is because once a person reaches a conclusion, they can be prone to becoming close-minded to new ideas. After all, the matter is resolved—or so they think.

There is another interesting lesson to be learned from Monk and the like. Sometimes all of the details point towards a suspect, but there is clearly no motive for the crime. Again, the great detective intuitively knows that while the trees say one thing, the forest says quite another.

BLACK AND WHITE READING

We sometimes come across Bible passages that "seem off." Thus far, I've referred to these moments as "red flags" that cause the reader to stop and ask questions (recall, for instance, the red flags of alarm while reading the story of Lot and his daughters in Genesis 19).

But unlike Monk who was never afraid to think for himself, sometimes we're hesitant to question the accepted narrative, or the text which is right before our eyes. After all, as some say, "The text is in black and white. Just read it. Isn't that clear enough?" This statement, while seemingly true, is a wrong assumption. Of course, Monk knew that too. I can hear him saying, "He's the guy. Just because he has an alibi, doesn't mean he wasn't in two places at once (so to speak)."

Proof-texting is another way to describe black and white reading. This takes place when a person focuses on a single verse or two to prove the argument at hand.

Some insist that, "The Bible says it and that's good enough for me." This conveys the idea that words are void of context and do not require interpretation. The absurdity of this is illustrated in a graphic[39] I found years ago. In the center of the graphic are the words, "Put your hands in the air." Those words probably convey an initial mental picture to you. The problem is that your image may or may not be correct. Is this placed within the context of a bank robber, a music DJ, a preacher's exhortation, or a mom who is trying to get her child to take off their shirt?

Thinking a verse in the Bible is very clear and plain is not the same as it actually being so. The biblical examples that may be presented are endless. Consider the following:

- Matthew 18:9a says, "If your eye causes you to stumble, pluck it out."

  But we don't believe in such mutilation of the body.

- Romans 8:13a says, "If you are living according to the flesh, you must die."

  But we don't believe in either murder or suicide.

- Romans 16:16a says, "Greet one another with a holy kiss."

  But we prefer to shake hands or hug one another.

- 1 Corinthians 14:34a says, "Let the women keep silent in the churches."

  But women are allowed to talk in our churches.

- 1 Timothy 2:8 says, "I want the men in every place to pray, lifting up holy hands."

  But this only tends to happen in churches that are more charismatic or expressive, and even then, not every single time they pray.

- 1 Timothy 5:3, 9 says, "Honor widows who are widows indeed . . . Let a widow be put on the list only if she is not less than sixty years old."

  But I never heard of a church that has such a list.

- Colossians 3:22a says, "Slaves, in all things obey those who are your masters."

  But we believe slavery is wrong.

- Galatians 2:21b says, "Christ died for nothing."

  But we certainly do not believe this.

- Ephesians 4:17 says, "You must no longer live as the Gentiles do."

  But should I live as a Jew?

- Philippians 2:21 says, "Everyone looks out for his own interests."

  But should I be selfish and apathetic?

- Matthew 5:43 says, "Love your neighbor and hate your enemy."

But is hate really a Christian virtue?

- Psalm 10:1 says, "Why, O lord, do you stand far off? Why do you hide yourself in times of trouble?"

But isn't the lord always near?

- Psalm 12:2 says, "Everyone lies to his neighbor."

But isn't lying wrong?

- And my personal favorite, Proverbs 6:4 says, "Give no sleep to your eyes, nor slumber to your eyelids."

But doesn't my body require sleep?

Some of the above examples may jump out immediately as being taken out of context. Something in us pulls back from statements like "pluck your eye out" and we intuitively know we have to put it in context to make the meaning clearer. Other texts, however, are not so obvious. We might not even give them a second thought if someone quoted them to us to prove a point they wanted to make. Sadly, some purposely do this kind of proof texting to convince us of their positions. But there is also the problem when we unknowingly do it and argue about our poor interpretations. "Black and white" reading is often the devil's instrument for creating division in the church.

All biblical texts have one thing in common—you can't "just read them" and understand them without sound interpretive method. They cannot be treated as black and white statements that must be true; they must always be placed within a proper context (literary, historical, cultural, etc.). It's context that enables us to see beyond the black and white of the text.

LITERARY CONTEXT

Due to social media, we're more familiar with literary context than we have ever been. Story after story features a headline ripped out of context to serve as "clickbait." Once opened, the article often tells the very opposite of what the headline led us to believe.

In the world of hermeneutics, it's said that "context is king." In other words, before the interpreter rushes off to conclusions, or even to other interpretive methods, literary context should be considered.

Any hermeneutics textbook[40] worth a grain of salt will devote considerable space to literary context. It's the most important skill every Bible student must master. Here are the nine steps I teach my students to follow when studying context:

1. *Text*—What is the biblical text you are studying? It could be just one verse, but read, at minimum, the complete chapter before you do anything else.

2. *Immediate Context*—Place the text into a paragraph. This is a bit subjective, as evidenced by the fact that translations don't always agree as to where the paragraphs begin or end. Nevertheless, do your best or just follow your translation of choice.

3. *The Point*—Ask, "What's the point of the paragraph?" This helps you articulate the most important thing being stated. Though Step 2 suggested you zoom back into the paragraph level, there are times when the paragraph may not help you determine the main point (John 8:31–33 is a good example of this). In such cases, you may need to broaden your scope again. This is why some scholars extend their definition of "immediate context" beyond the paragraph. I, however, do not think it always needs to be that broad. Still, whether it be paragraph or chapter, or even something further, you really don't know the point without reading the complete discussion. So be aware, the last thing you want to do is press a point onto a paragraph when you have not read everything. This is absolutely crucial.

4. *The Topics*—Ask, "What are some of the topics being mentioned?" Identifying these will be of value later. Don't just look for key words but think in terms of issues implicit in the text (e.g., if the text said, "he was talking to God," then prayer would be a topic).

5. *Surrounding Context*—Read the text that comes both "before" and "after" (don't think in terms of chapters). You want to figure out where this topic or discussion both began and ended. I like to think in terms of "shifting gears" with a manual transmission. Written documents shift gears, moving from one topic to another all the time. Find the complete discussion that involves your gear. Now, how does the text fit into the complete topic being discussed?

6. *Book Context*—Ask, "How does the text fit into the book as a whole?" This is where remembering what you learned in Steps 3–4 becomes helpful. That means, you have to read the entire book, preferably in one sitting.[41]

7. *Author or Genre Context*—Ask, "How does the text fit into the author's writings as a whole?" You may think of how John, for example, wrote

The Gospel According to John, 1–3 John, and *Revelation.* In other words, does your author often speak about the point and topics you identified in Steps 3–4? Sometimes, of course, the author only wrote one book. In these situations, it's helpful to think in terms of genre for comparisons on the topic in play. For example, Matthew only wrote one book, but there are four total gospels, so think about those.

8. *Testament Context*—Now think in terms of the entire testament. If it's a New Testament text you're examining, then this step would consider New Testament teaching.

9. *Biblical Context*—The final step is to consider the text within the full scope of the Bible. Sometimes we neglect this step because we falsely believe that the two testaments are disjointed and have little in common. For example, as Burge[42] explains succinctly, too many make the mistake of thinking "grace" is only a New Testament concept. What a dreadful error.

Now let's take Philippians 4:13 and walk through the process. Here, Paul gave us a favorite refrigerator slogan: "I can do all things through Him *(Christ)* who strengthens me."

1. *Text*—Philippians 4:13

2. *Immediate Context*—I'm going to say it's 4:10–13.

3. *The Point*—I'll say, "God is with Paul in all circumstances."

4. *The Topics*—Some of the topics are: concern, living in need or prosperity, contentment, suffering, and the Holy Spirit (the one who strengthens).

5. *Surrounding Context*—I'm going to say it's 4:4–19. My reasoning for backing up to verse 4 is that "rejoiced" (v. 10) somewhat links to verse 4 and following. Paul can rejoice because he can do all things through him. The "after" may extend to verse 19 because it seems to reinforce verse 13. Also, the "suffering" of verse 12 links to "affliction" in verse 14. Furthermore, Paul's "needs" (v. 16) link to his needs experienced in verse 12. You may want to note that God uses people (vv. 15–16) to meet needs.

6. *Book Context*—The key words in Philippians are "rejoice" (9x) and "joy" (7x). Unity is also crucial and is brought up in three chapters (1:27; 2:2, 14; 4:2). Opposition is mentioned in 1:15, 17, 28; 3:2, 18. As we consider these themes and how they may relate to our text, we might summarize as follows: Paul can rejoice in spite of any circumstance (he

is imprisoned as he writes) and the Christians at Philippi have pulled together (unity) to help meet his needs.

7. *Author Context*—Think about Acts 9–28 and all of Paul's letters. As I reflect on our main point, "God is with Paul in all circumstances," my mind immediately drifts to both the shipwreck Paul survived in Acts 27, and the stoning he suffered in Acts 14:19. The stoning was so severe, they thought he was dead, but God was with him! Of course, these examples are just the tip of the iceberg.

8. *Testament Context*—How do we see God being present with others in the New Testament? Going back to Acts, just think of how Peter and the apostles were jailed in Acts 5. But "during the night an angel of the Lord opened the gates of the prison" (v. 19). The examples are numerous.

9. *Biblical Context*—Just think about how God was with Noah, Joseph, Moses, Daniel, etc.

While the process I've described may vary slightly from methodologies suggested by others, there's nothing here that will surprise anyone who has studied hermeneutics. Still, the process of studying various layers of context (what I sometimes just call "layering") does help us bring everything into focus. Virtually every step takes you beyond the initial point of interest, whether it be a text like Philippians 4:13 or even the paragraph of 4:10–13.

One must see beyond the trees of verses 10–13 and into the forest before them (i.e., the entire biblical context). Study that fails to ever get to Steps 8–9 falls short, yet this is often a problem. Interpreters sometimes get fixated on a text and simply can't see past those few words. Again, they may say, "It's in black and white. Just read it; it's very clear." We must, however, always see beyond the verse, and even its immediate context, and go exploring in the woods.

A CASE STUDY—1 TIMOTHY 2:12

1 Timothy 2:12 is a perfect place to model this type of exploration. There are two primary branches of thought regarding the role of women and church leadership. Complementarians believe men should be the sole leaders of the church. Egalitarians, on the other hand, believe women should not be excluded from serving the lord in leadership roles. While this book is not the place to discuss the many differences of opinion between the two groups, this is a valid case study to include here, as one of the biggest issues

is grounded in hermeneutics, specifically seeing only the trees and not the entire forest.

As a basis for their argument, complementarians often point to 1 Timothy 2:12. Paul told Timothy, "I do not allow a woman to teach or exercise authority over a man, but to remain quiet." While the text may seem very clear, it is not.

In *Beyond Reasonable Doubt*, I discussed a whole list of issues within the passage that show it is not a simple "black and white" text. That list included the following items:

- The background of Ephesus—specifically the Temple of Artemis and the role of women at Ephesus

- The chiastic[43] structure of the letter of 1 Timothy—specifically that the "submissiveness of women and their witness" (1 Tim 2:9–15) parallels "submissiveness of slaves and their witness" (1 Tim 6:1–2).

- The literary context—specifically that false teaching is a problem in the church at Ephesus (1 Tim 1:3–4, 6–8; 2:14; 4:1–5, 7; 6:3–5, 20) and the women are being used to worsen the matter (1 Tim 2:9–15; 3:11; 4:7; 5:13–15; 2 Tim 3:6).

- The command is to "learn." While emphasis is placed on verse 12, the only imperative in chapter 2 is found in verse 11 where it says, "A woman must quietly receive instruction with entire submissiveness." The imperative is the Greek word *manthanō*, which means "to learn." While the NASB translates this "receive instruction," both the NIV and ESV say "learn."

- Did Paul actually say, "authority over a man"? He may have actually said "authority over a husband" (as the NIV points out in its notes). The word Paul used was *aner*, his normal word of choice when speaking of a marital context. He could have said *arsen* (male) or *anthropos* (any person or mankind) but he did not. 1 Timothy 2:13–15 is clearly a marital context as it speaks of Adam, Eve and children. Understanding 1 Timothy 2:12 as husband and wife would also be consistent with 1 Corinthians 14:34–35.[44]

- Did Paul actually say, "exercise authority"? The word *authenteō* is only used once in the entire New Testament and its meaning is uncertain. "The simple fact that Paul could have chosen to use *exousiazō*, *kyrieuō*, or *proistēmi* cannot be ignored. That is exactly what he did in every other passage he wrote that addressed authority, jurisdiction, rule and the like."[45]

- The discussion in verses 13–14 surrounding Adam and Eve does not constitute a "creation principle." Paul uses this as an illustration concerning deception. Like Eve, the women at Ephesus have been deceived. Complementarians often point to Eve being deceived as evidence that females are more deceivable and thus, should not lead. Such logic is clearly flawed, unless one would also admit that like Adam who disobeyed God, all males are bent on disobedience and cannot be trusted to obey God.

- Women are not being permanently restricted to the home (2:15). "Since the women at Ephesus were weak and easily captivated by false teachers (2 Tim 3:6), they needed to stay busy (not idle, 5:13), attending to their homes (5:14). This would help them keep their attention where it belonged—on Christ."[46] Verse 15 must be interpreted within this context.

1 Timothy 2:12 is anything but a "black and white" text. But when readers remain fixated on texts which seem so clear, they have difficulty seeing the forest before them. So, let's work through this text using the "layering" method described earlier to see if we can get past the trees.

1. Text

1 Timothy 2:12

2. Immediate Context

1 Timothy 2:8–15. I back up to verse 8 because it begins with the transition word "Therefore." While some translations such as the ESV omit the word, it is present in Greek. Verse 8 says, "Therefore, I want the men in every place to pray, lifting up holy hands, without wrath and dissension."

3. The Point

As explained earlier, we often need to broaden our scope (or "zoom out" again) to determine the point. With "Therefore" standing at the outset of verse 8, it is impossible to ascertain the point of verses 8–15 without reading what precedes it. Indeed, 1 Timothy 2:1–7 must be read first. The point I land on will probably surprise you. Paul's real point of 2:8–15 seems to be something like, "Men and women alike are to live *godly lives* that promote *unity and truth*, and *point others toward God.*"

This may be perceived as an unconventional interpretation because we often stare exclusively at verses 9–15. For example, the NASB misleads by placing a heading ("Women Instructed") directly above verse 9. But as both the NASB and ESV note, verse 9 begins with the word "Likewise," drawing connection to the previous verse. It is clear that the immediate context is 2:8–15, not 2:9–15. In other words, this is not a section about women. It is a continuation of larger thought and includes instructions to both men and women—remember the "therefore."

Notice how the train of thought reads with these layers in mind (emphasis and insertion mine): "*Therefore* [i.e., in light of what I just said], I want the men in every place to pray, lifting up holy hands, without wrath and dissension. *Likewise*, I want women to . . ."

Why do I include "unity and truth" as part of the point? Note that verse 8 (speaking of the men) ends by saying "without wrath and dissension." While verses 9–10 address modesty and how outward appearance does not equal godliness, it also probably says something about breaking down the class differences within the church (a unity issue). Verses 11–15 may also be seen as a unity concern. Regardless of where we land on gender roles, it is clear that disturbance is occurring in the church, as the women have been deceived and now need to be silenced. Sound teaching (truth) will help create a unified church.

Why do I say, "godly lives"? The word "godliness" is noticeable in verse 10 (and also 2:2). Also, as one thinks about how deceptive teaching wreaks havoc on the Christian life, it seems reasonable to see Paul's concern for godly living. Verse 15 serves to reinforce this concern. Furthermore, Christian lives that promote unity must be seen within a context of godliness. I have to admit, however, that due to my previous knowledge of Paul's repeated use of the word "godliness" in 1 Timothy, I have presuppositions that could be impacting my interpretation.

Why do I say, "point others toward God"? 1 Timothy 2:1–4 shows a concern for the well-being of others, specifically that they are "saved" (v. 4). Seeing men pray (2:8) points people to God. Paul's concern of women taking attention away from outward appearance and instead towards their good works (2:9–10) is a means to point others toward God. Furthermore, correct biblical teaching (2:11–14) always points others towards God.

4. The Topics

The main topics are: unity, prayer, godliness, witness, apparel, learning, truth, teaching, and deception. The omission of gender roles may appear alarming or even shocking, but once the point of the immediate context is established (live godly lives that promote unity and point others toward God), the previous assumption surrounding gender roles somewhat fades into the background. With this being a letter (the genre), we know that Paul is addressing specific situations to which Timothy must respond. Paul is trying to solve a problem, not write doctrine. Thus, Paul's directions should not be taken as universally prescriptive for all churches. With his chief concerns being godly living, unity, and witness, it begins to seem unnatural to press the topic of gender roles.

5. Surrounding Context

1 Timothy 2:1–3:16 seems to be the complete surrounding context. Again, the "Therefore" at the outset of 2:8 reveals that the previous section (vv. 1–7) is linked to verses 8–15. In this section (vv. 1–7), Paul encourages prayer for all people. His concerns surround *secular leaders* who will allow Christians to live their lives in an undisturbed godly manner. He also prays for all men, as God desires all to come to the knowledge of truth. He concludes the section by talking about the ultimate truth, Christ who gave himself as a ransom for all. Of this truth, Paul has been made a teacher.

Paul's concern for restoring order (due to disarray in the church outlined in 2:9–15) continues into chapter 3. While there are questions regarding chapter 3 (e.g., women or deaconess issues surrounding 3:11),[47] we will forgo that discussion and get to the point—that Paul begins describing what *godly leaders* look like. Note how Paul wraps this up: "I write so that you will know how one ought to conduct himself in the household of God, which is the church of the living God, the pillar and support of the truth" (3:15).

Paul's overall point to 2:1–3:16 is probably something like, "Godly leaders teach truth, which dispels false teaching and promotes godly living, unity, and effective Christian witness." Remember, Jesus is the ultimate truth (2:4–6), Paul is a teacher of the truth (2:7), and godly leaders (3:1–13) must also teach truth (3:2). At present, however, the church at Ephesus has both a "teacher" and "truth" problem (2:11–15). The women have been deceived (2:14) and are propagating false teaching (2:11–12).

It's of no surprise that Paul puts a halt to this. The real shock is that he tells them to "learn" (2:11), the same point Paul makes in 1 Corinthians

14:35. This is shocking because there was little emphasis placed on women learning in antiquity. Remember this is an imperative, so Paul does not suggest that they learn, he commands it. He essentially says, "You must learn." Given the context, this isn't a command to learn for the sake of learning. It is a command to learn because learning precedes teaching.

6. Book Context

One of the clear purposes of the letter is to address the false teaching that Paul is contending with at Ephesus. Not only is this a prevalent theme throughout (1:3–4, 6–8; 2:14; 4:1–5, 7; 6:3–5, 20), but the letter also both begins and ends with the topic. It's of no surprise that Paul often mentions "teaching, teachers, teach" (11x), sometimes referring to the need for sound teaching.

The women at the church (mentioned frequently, 2:9–15; 3:11; 4:3–7; 5:3–16) were susceptible to false teaching. They (especially the young widows) appear to have been susceptible to ascetic teaching that devalued marriage (4:3), which is one of the reasons Paul tells the women to get married and bear children (5:14). In contrast to continuing in faith (2:15), when they choose sensual desires (5:6, 11) over Christ (5:11) they incur condemnation and set aside their faith (5:12) to follow Satan (5:15). In this context, it's less confusing to see Paul say, "women shall be preserved (both the NIV and ESV say, "saved") through the bearing of children" (2:15). Paul knew the women at Ephesus were weak and easily captivated by false teachers (2 Tim 3:6), but if they would stay busy (not idle, 5:13) attending to their homes (5:14) it would keep their attention from wandering to things like gossip and false teaching.

Paul often deals with three other primary issues: godliness, our witness, and being saved versus being lost. Each of these topics coincides with Paul's primary point of proclaiming Christ as the Savior of all men (4:9–11, also 1:1 and 2:3). Christians are to practice godliness and put forth a witness that is conducive to leading the lost to Christ, who died to save all men. With Jesus, the "Savior of all men" being the big point of the letter (see the chiasm of 1 Timothy),[48] it seems important to note that this is one of the three "trustworthy statements" Paul highlights in the letter.

"Godliness" (9x) is a crucial word in the letter and it must be understood within the framework of our witness, the most repeated theme of the letter. In fact, reference to the Christian witness is found within every chapter of the letter (1:16; 2:2, 9–10; 3:2–16; 4:12, 15; 5:4–10, 25; 6:1–2, 12). The Christian witness is very personal to Paul as he sees his own life to be an "example for those who would believe" in Christ for eternal life (1:16). And, of course, the Christian witness is to do just that—lead people to Christ. Thus, it is hardly surprising that when Paul speaks of godliness and the Christian witness, he also often speaks of salvation.

7. Author Context

Paul wrote thirteen letters, but because he wrote a *second letter to Timothy*, it is the first place to begin. In that letter, Paul notes that he is a teacher (2 Tim 1:11) and tells Timothy to "retain the standard of sound words which you have heard from me" (2 Tim 1:13). Paul elaborates by saying, "The things which you have heard from me in the presence of many witnesses, entrust these to faithful men[49] [NIV says, "people"] who will be able to teach others also" (2 Tim 2:2). Paul mentions how "worldly and empty chatter" leads to ungodliness (2 Tim 2:14, 16–17) and admonishes Timothy to "accurately handle the word of truth" (2 Tim 2:15). He follows his concern for godly living (2 Tim 2:19–22) by saying, "Refuse foolish and ignorant speculations, knowing that they produce quarrels. The Lord's bond-servant must not be quarrelsome, but be kind to all, able to teach . . ." (2 Tim 2:23–24). Chapter 3 provides important background information that concerns our text in 1 Timothy 2:9–15. Paul talks about the kind of men who should be avoided and says, "For among them are those who enter into households and captivate weak women weighed down with sins, led on by various impulses, always learning, and never able to come to the knowledge of the truth" (2 Tim 3:6–7). While speaking about the "last days" (3:1), this sounds like Paul is using an example from something that has already happened. *In summary*, Paul does not broach the topic of female leadership in 2 Timothy. His primary concern, as related to 1 Timothy, is that false teachers (2:14–3:9) stand in opposition to the "truth" (6x—2:15, 18, 25; 3:7–8; 4:4). They must be combated through godly "people" who are able to teach others.

With *Titus* being one of the three "pastoral epistles" (1 Tim, 2 Tim, and Titus), it is also of particular interest. Titus 1:5–9 echoes much of 1 Timothy 3:1–7, expressing concerns for both godliness and sound doctrine. Paul mentions "rebellious men, empty talkers and deceivers . . . who must be silenced because they are upsetting whole families" (Titus 1:10–11). At the outset of chapter 2, Paul tells Titus to speak things of "sound doctrine" (Titus 2:1). He continues by saying that older women are not to be "malicious gossips . . . teaching what is good so that they may encourage the young women to love their husbands, to love their children, . . . being subject to their own husbands, so that the word of God will not be dishonored"

(Titus 2:3–5). This brings to mind both 1 Timothy 5:13–15 and 2:15. Note that Paul also tells "bondslaves to be subject to their own masters in everything" (Titus 2:9). Paul's pressing concern is godly living that produces good deeds (Titus 2:7–8, 12, 14; 3:1–2, 8, 14). *In summary*, like 1 Timothy 3, Paul appeals to godly men to provide sound doctrine. He encourages godly living that produces fruit and gives several examples of how that may be lived out by different groups (e.g., older men, older women, young men, bondslaves—Titus 2:1–9). Paul adheres to the cultural expectation of his day (e.g., the men are elders, wives are subject to their husbands, slaves are subject to their masters). If we take Paul's instructions about male elders (Titus 1:5–6) as a universal rule, then we should also endorse the other hierarchies mentioned, like the slave-master relationship (Titus 2:9), as such. There is nothing in the text to suggest that one is a universal expectation, while the others are only cultural. Wherever you land on one, you must follow with all.

Because Timothy was in Ephesus, Paul's letter to the Ephesians seems like the next logical place to explore.[50] Paul does not mention "women" in the letter but does spend considerable time discussing both wives and husbands in 5:22–33. Given that the content is similar but not exactly parallel, several things must be kept in mind while examining Ephesians in relation to our text. First, because Ephesians speaks of the marital relationship, it cannot be argued that anything set forth can automatically be transferred to a church leadership context. Second, while Ephesians 5:22 says, "Wives, be subject to your own husbands," it's been well documented that the word "submit" (or "subject") is not actually present in 5:22. The verb from verse 21 governs the phrase in verse 22. Verse 21 says, "and be subject to one another in the fear of Christ." "In other words, the true Christian ideal is that all Christians submit to one another anyway. Thus, while Paul never says husbands should submit to wives, it's implicit that mutual submission is always ideal."[51]

Third, though the text says that the "husband is the head of the wife" (5:23), the passage says nothing concerning who is in control or who has authority. While the depth of the image may be debated, at the least, we have an image of the two needing one another (one flesh, 5:28–29, 31, 33). Although it must be admitted that Paul draws similarity (5:23) in that the husband is the head of the wife, as Christ is the church, it's very interesting that Paul does not conclude by speaking of authority (as some expect). Instead, Paul finishes the sentence by saying, "He Himself being the Savior of the body" (5:23). This isn't exactly an image that communicates one being in charge over another. Instead, the image Paul fleshes out is of the one who sacrifices for his bride (5:25). Fourth, the culturally surprising statement is that Paul tells husbands to love their wives. Wives were commanded by both Roman and Jewish law to obey their husbands, but husbands were not required to love their wives. In commanding husbands to love their wives (4x in 5:25, 28, 33), "Paul gives new revolutionary meaning to man's role in marriage. Due to this important inclusion, this text was actually somewhat liberating to the wives of Paul's day."[52] *In summary*, there's nothing substantial in this text that would prohibit women from serving in church leadership roles.

Colossians has much in common with Ephesians, in particular, the section concerning the Greco-Roman household codes (Col 3:18–4:1 and Eph 5:22–6:9). Like Ephesians, Colossians does not mention women, only wives in 3:18–19. Verse 18 says, "Wives, be subject to your husbands, as is fitting in the Lord." The latter statement provides some Christian guardrails and points to the rights of the wives. And husbands are no longer to look at their wives as property, but they are to love their wives. Paul is pointing believers toward a higher ethic than their current cultural demands. Of interest is that Nympha (a female) hosted the Laodicean church in her home (Col 4:15). *In summary*, like Ephesians, there's nothing in this text that would prohibit women from serving in church leadership roles.

With 2 Timothy, Titus, Ephesians, and Colossians now examined, eight Pauline letters remain to consult. But because there is nothing in either *2 Corinthians* or *1 & 2 Thessalonians* that speaks to concerns about women and leadership, we have five letters left: Philippians, Galatians, Philemon, Romans, and 1 Corinthians.

In *Philippians*, Paul makes mention of two women: Euodia and Syntyche (4:2–3). These women "had struggled (*synathleo*) along with Paul for the sake of the gospel." *In summary*, these women were out on the front lines doing ministry.

Galatians contributes to the discussion when Paul gives us the "there is neither male nor female" statement in Galatians 3:28. But the statement does not stand in isolation. First, it must be understood within the context of the entire chapter, where Paul goes into great detail contrasting the Law and faith. And second, verses 26–29 have a great deal to consider. Paul says,

> 26 For you are all sons of God through faith in Christ Jesus.
> 27 For all of you who were baptized into Christ have clothed yourselves with Christ. 28 There is neither Jew nor Greek, there is neither slave nor free man, there is neither male nor female; for you are all one in Christ Jesus. 29 And if you belong to Christ, then you are Abraham's descendants, heirs according to promise.

Verse 26 tells us that through faith, all can become sons of God (and the figurative speech does not exclude females). Verse 27 reveals that all can be baptized into Christ. And verse 29 declares that all become the true seed of Abraham. Yes, all become sons, all can be baptized (unlike male circumcision), and all become heirs (previously, only males were heirs). Paul is breaking down all the privileged distinctions that once existed (being a Jew, being male, and being free). *In summary*, through faith in Christ, all are one and the playing field has been leveled.

The book of *Philemon* is a tremendous demonstration of the truth in Galatians 3:26–29. While Paul follows cultural expectations and sends the runaway slave Onesimus back to Philemon, he essentially tells Philemon the jig is up! He submits a striking challenge: How can you be a master/slave at home but then go to church and be equals as "brothers" (v. 16)? Just as Paul and Philemon are partners, so are Philemon and Onesimus (v. 17). *In summary*, the power of the gospel breaks down inequalities that exist in a sinful world.

The females Paul mentions in chapter 16 of *Romans* are relevant to our discussion. Paul lists twenty-seven people in this chapter, with eight (30 percent) being women. Among those cited are: "Phoebe the deacon (v. 1), Priscilla the teacher (v. 3) and Junia the possible apostle (v. 7).[53] The other five women just get lost to the modern reader, as do most of the men."[54] But deserving attention, I list them here: Mary ("worked hard," v. 6), Tryphaena and Tryphosa ("workers in the lord," v. 12), Persis ("the beloved, who has worked hard in the lord," v. 12), and Julia (no specific comment, v. 15). *In summary*, these are significant women doing significant ministry.

Finally, we have come to *1 Corinthians*. Because Paul has a great deal to say about women in this letter, it is of utmost importance. Before I move to the primary texts of interest, it's significant to point out that Chloe (1 Cor 1:11) may have hosted a church in her home and Stephanas (1 Cor 16:15) may actually be a female.[55] But placing those aside, let's move first to 1 Corinthians 14:34–35. It says, "The women are to keep silent in the churches; for they are not permitted to speak, but are to subject themselves, just as the Law also says. If they desire to learn anything, let them ask their own husbands at home; for it is improper for a woman to speak in church." There are three points to make about this passage. First, there is a chiasm[56] present that shows silence is not the primary point at hand. Rather, "learn" lies at the center of the chiasm and serves as Paul's driving point. Second, you'll be hard pressed to find a person today who believes that Paul is prohibiting women from ever speaking at church. Even in this same book, "Paul allows women to pray and prophesy (1 Cor 11:5), does not exclude women from spiritual gifts (1 Cor 12:1–11, 28–31; 14:1–32) and adamantly encourages body ministry (1 Cor 12:12–31)."[57] Third, we need to observe the repetition in chapter 14. The words "edify" and "edification" are key as they are used six total times. In summary here, "It is apparent that the women are commanded to remain silent because their words are not edifying the body of Christ."[58]

I've left 1 Corinthians 11 for last because on many levels, verses 3–16 are simply difficult to interpret. In fact, Blomberg says, "This passage is probably the most complex, controversial, and opaque of any text of comparable length in the New Testament."[59]

> The complexity of this text makes it a prime passage for playing textual ping-pong. Complementarians point to verse 3 which says, 'man is the head of woman.' And in turn, egalitarians look at verse 5 which indicates women both prayed and prophesied. Complementarians then quote verse 8 which says woman came from man. But, of course, egalitarians then point out verse 12 which says, 'man has his birth through the woman.' But finally, it would seem that complementarians win the day by noting that verse 7 says 'woman is the glory of man.'
>
> The problem with this typical ping-pong scenario is twofold. The Apostle Paul did not write statements that stand in opposition to one another. Furthermore, our goal is not to win a ping-pong game, but to come to an understanding of what Paul meant by these words. It bears repeating that even Peter confessed that Paul's words were sometimes difficult to understand (2 Pet 3:15–16).[60]

While I have said much about these texts in the past,[61] I'm not hesitant to admit that I have many questions and do not feel certain about some of my own conclusions. Having said that, the following issues should be considered.

Paul's statement in verse 3 ("the man is the head of a woman") can, and probably should, be translated as "husband" and "wife," as the ESV and at least twelve other translations do.

Also, in this same verse, should "head" (*kephale*) be understood as "having authority over" as complementarians insist, or can it mean "source" or "origin" as some egalitarians suggest? If "husband" and "wife" are the correct rendering, then we are back to a marital context (Eph 5), making the meaning of *kephale* insignificant (as far as the issue of whether women can serve in church leadership). Also, if *kephale* does indeed mean "head" here, one must notice that "body" is absent (unlike Eph 5). This seems curious, but at the same time, Paul's point would govern how far he wants to take the image. With context being king, we must heavily note what Paul says in verses 8–12. Here, Paul speaks of the woman coming from man and how both the woman and man are dependent upon each other (man being born of woman). He concludes by saying "all things originate from God."

It could be that verse 12 echoes what he previously said in verse 3. However, in the midst of this "source/origin" language of verses 8–9 and 11–12, is verse 10 which speaks about the woman having authority on her head. Admittedly, it's a head scratcher and serves to prove the complex nature of this entire passage. But the puzzling statement may be solved in translation. While both the NASB and ESV insert the words "a symbol," the phrase is not present in the Greek text. A more correct translation may be found in both the NIV and KJV, which respectively say, "woman ought to have authority over her head" and "woman ought to have power on her head." Once again, however, this may only complicate matters because, in light of verses 8–9, the interpretation just described doesn't seem to make sense. I must admit that this passage drives me crazy and leaves me feeling confused. I can't help but wonder if Paul first addresses cultural expectations in verses 4–6 (concerns over praying, prophesying, head covered or not, head shaved, and hair cut off) but eventually moves to the higher truth of verses 11–12. Note that verse 11 begins with "However" ("Nevertheless" in both the NIV and ESV). Following the conjunction, Paul addresses the complete interdependence of both man and woman, with God being the originator of all.

As a final point, verse 7 is not saying that women were not created in the image of God. Genesis 1:26–27 is clear in that both man and woman were created in God's image, and that they were both to "rule." *In summary*, while 1 Corinthians 11 can be difficult to understand, Paul does not state that women should be prohibited from church leadership roles.

8. New Testament Context

Having reviewed Pauline material, fourteen books remain. That people seldom bring Jesus (the gospels) into this conversation continues to amaze me. It would almost seem they think he has nothing to say on the matter. Yet, we find Jesus' language and actions do indeed speak to his view of women and their importance in his Kingdom. First, imperative to Jesus is that leadership is not about power, but rather about attitudes. Jesus' criteria does not revolve around gender; he's more concerned with love and sacrificial service. Second, Luke 4:16–21 is an important text, as women are certainly included in the captive downtrodden that he has come to set free. His statements surrounding divorce clearly show that they have the same rights as men in his counter-culture teaching. And while women were often viewed as sexual objects in antiquity, Jesus views them as people.[62] Third, Jesus acknowledges that women have faith equal to that of men. In fact, in fourteen gospel passages where faith is applauded, six refer to men and five refer to women (three times faith is attributed to a crowd). Fourth,

> Jesus did not exclude women from learning and preaching the gospel. In fact, He gave His full endorsement and commissioned them to do so. That is clearly due to the fact that within the kingdom of God men and women have equal status, equal opportunity to learn, equal acceptance by God, and equal ability to model and use great faith.[63]

In support, one may think of the following:

- Elizabeth, righteous and filled with the Holy Spirit (Luke 1:6, 41)

- Mary, favored one (Luke 1:28)

- Traveling disciples (Luke 8:1–3)

- Mary and Martha as disciples (Luke 10:38–42). Mary sits at Jesus' feet, the posture of someone being formally educated, and Jesus commends her for it.

- Samaritan woman, a preacher proclaiming Christ (John 4:29, 39)

- Women at the tomb, preachers of the good news (Matt 28:10; Mark 16:7; Luke 24:9; John 21:17). Jesus first appears to the women (Matt 28:10; John 20:14) and they are entrusted with telling of the resurrected Christ.

Fifth, Jesus uses female imagery to refer to God. In Matthew 23:37 Jesus speaks of Jerusalem and laments, "How often I wanted to gather your children together, the way a hen gathers her chicks under her wings, and you were unwilling" (see also Luke 13:34). And in the parable of the lost coin (Luke 15:8–10), Jesus uses a woman to find the coin, with a clear comparison being made to God who finds the lost. Finally, the Great Commission (Matt 28:19–20) assumes both men and women are to share in this responsibility. We're told to "make disciples," "baptize," and "teach."

Acts is significant to the discussion. In Acts 1:14, we're told that the women were among those in the upper room with the disciples. When Pentecost arrived, the women were among those filled with the Holy Spirit (Acts 2:1–4). When Peter appeals to Joel's prophecy in Acts 2:17–18, he says that "sons and daughters will prophesy" and that God's servants are both "men and women." Grenz says that Luke specifically mentions "women at each stage . . . of the church's expansion: Jerusalem (Acts 5:14), Samaria

(8:12) and the cities of the Roman world like Philippi (16:13–15), Thessalonica (17:4), Berea (17:12), Athens (17:34) and Corinth (18:2)."[64] Witherington concurs saying, as the author of Acts, "Luke chronicles the progress of women as part of the progress and effects of the Christian gospel."[65] In Acts 21:9, we read of Philip's four virgin daughters who were prophetesses. Staton speculates, "Mentioning their virginity may have been Luke's way to emphasize that a woman does not have to be paired with a man to have significant leadership ministry in the early Church."[66] Finally, Luke recalls three notable women who should be mentioned: Tabitha, Mary, mother of John Mark, and Lydia. Tabitha (9:36–42) was called a "disciple." Mary appears to have hosted a church in her home (12:12–17). Lydia also became a church host (16:40). What is clear in Acts, is that women were significant in the development of the church and they helped spread the gospel message.

We call chapter 11 of *Hebrews*, the "faith chapter." Among the heroes that are credited with faith are Sarah (11:11), women who "received back their dead by resurrection" (11:35), and Rahab (11:31). *James* also mentions Rahab, using her as a model of how faith accompanies works (2:25).

1 Peter addresses the priesthood of all believers (2:5, 9), as does *Revelation* 1:6 (see also Rev 5:10; 20:6). Imagine that, women are now part of the priesthood that minister before God. That's a powerful image that breaks down barriers. Revelation 2:20 makes mention of Jezebel. It's interesting to note that she is scolded because she teaches immorality and leads others astray, not because she is female.

In 1 Peter 3:1–7, there is an example of how Sarah was submissive to Abraham. Here, Peter tells wives to be submissive to their husbands (3:1, 5). Since, once again, this is framed within a marital context, it has no impact on gender roles in ministry. Nevertheless, before one gets too carried away with Peter's statements (e.g., Sarah even called Abraham "lord"—v. 6), consider that proper Christian living is also at the forefront of Peter's mind. The word "holy" (7x when not used in the phrase "Holy Spirit") is key. Peter tells us that because God is holy, the church is a holy priesthood, and a holy nation. Therefore, we are to be holy in our behavior (1:15). As Peter addresses Christian living, he also uses the word "behavior" (5x in 1:15; 2:12; 3:1–2, 16), "conduct" (1:17), and phrases such as "doing what is right" (2:14–15, 20; 3:6, 17; 4:19). The word "submit" or "submissive" (4x) is also noticeable and serves to show us that a good witness can impact those not living for Christ (2:12; 3:1).

Finally, *2 John* begins with John greeting the "chosen lady." While John could be referring to a local church (which verse 13 seems to support), there are at least four reasons for believing this refers to an actual person.[67]

9. Biblical Context—Persons of interest include:

- Eve (Helper, Gen 2:18, 20)—The word "helper" (*ezer*) is also used thirteen times in reference to God being our helper. Furthermore, it is often used in a military sense (i.e., one coming to "help" in battle) and is seldom used in a subordinate sense.

- Sarah (Partner in Faith)—Besides being commended for faith in Hebrews 11:11, we're told in Genesis 21:12 that Abraham listened to Sarah (and at God's command). She is so significant, that even her death is mentioned (Gen 23:1–2).

- Miriam (Prophetess, Exod 15:20)—Numbers 12:2 says that God spoke through Moses, Aaron, and Miriam.

- Rahab (Model of Faith and Works, Heb 11:31 and Jas 2:25)

- Deborah (Prophetess and Judge, Judg 4:4)—The statement some make about Deborah only leading because God couldn't find a man is outlandish. First, Hebrews 11:32–33 applauds Barak's faith. And yet, Deborah instructed him (Judg 4:6–7). Second, even if the statement were true, it would still say that God is willing to use women in ministry.

- Jael (Key Figure in War, Judg 4)—God used Jael to take care of business (Judg 4:23) and verses 24–27 are a song in honor of her.

- Manoah's Wife (Believed, Judg 13)—God sends the angel to Manoah's wife and she comes across as the person with more discernment and faith in this story.

- Abigail (Discernment, 1 Sam 25)—Abigail offers advice to David and prevents the shedding of blood. In response, David says, "blessed be your discernment and blessed are you" (1 Sam 25:32–33).

- A Wise Woman (2 Sam 20:16)—The city people listened to her, making it seem as if she had some type of leadership in the town.

- Huldah (Prophetess, 2 Kgs 22:14)—King Josiah ordered Hilkiah and others to go "inquire of the lord" and they went to Huldah. They could have consulted qualified men such as Jeremiah, Zephaniah, or Habakkuk, but they chose to consult a woman.

- Esther (Heroine Queen)—The courageous Esther led the Jews in fasting (4:16), a fast that clearly played a part in saving the Jews from Haman's plan to destroy them. Also, Esther is written about 150 years after Daniel, and the writer shows eleven parallels to the book, probably to show that God was working in the background while using a woman.

- Heralds of Good News (Isa 40:9)—"Bearer" is a feminine participle and this text may not be referring to a city as the bearer, as some translations indicate. It may very well be a person, given that Jerusalem is in no position to proclaim good news (41:27)—they need to hear it. Psalm 68:11 also speaks about "women who proclaim the good tidings."

- An Excellent Woman (Prov 31:10–31)—She was a businesswoman who also managed her home. This doesn't portray a woman who needs a male telling her what to do.

- Prophetesses and More—Isaiah's wife is called a prophetess (Isa 8:3). Noadiah was a false prophet, not because she is female, but because she did not speak on behalf of the lord (Neh 6:14). Ezekiel 13 identifies seven characteristics of false prophets, gender not being mentioned. In addition to being prophetesses, "women were allowed to be Nazarites (Num 6:2), served with priestly functions at festivals (Deut 12:12, 18), experienced theophanies (Gen 3:13; 16:8; 18:9; Judg 13:3), served the tabernacle (Exod 38:8), could associate with men (Gen 24:10–27) and had free access to the house of the lord" (1 Sam 1:7).[68]

A few final points should be made about biblical context. First, "The relational dynamic within the Godhead (between Father, Son and Holy Spirit) is, in some mysterious fashion, interconnected with the plurality within mankind (male and female)."[69] Second, God is not a gendered being; He is Spirit (John 4:24).

> Although the majority of the time God is described through masculine images, God is described to us through various metaphorical images (masculine, feminine and animalistic) to help us understand His nature. There are at least eighteen passages which portray God with feminine images (e.g., as a mother who gives birth, groans in labor, nurses a child, cares for children and provides comfort). The Holy Spirit may even be thought of in a feminine sense in Genesis 1:2, since "moving over the surface of the waters" closely resembles the hovering of a mother eagle in Deuteronomy 32:11. Some maintain that since Jesus was male, it proves God is male. This is flawed logic, for Jesus was also Jewish but no one would dare attribute a Jewish ethnicity to God. Others deny that the "Father" and the "Son" are metaphors and thus, say they speak to God's inherent maleness. Yet, "Father" and "Son" must be metaphors unless we believe Jesus is a literal offspring of God (in a sense that the Son did not exist before the incarnation). That Jesus speaks of His "Father" in no way proves

God is male. Father is a metaphorical image to help us see that God wants to have relationship with us. Jesus could not call God His mother, for He already had an earthly mother. Furthermore, when Jesus speaks of His Father in heaven, he does not do so to indicate God is male; He speaks of His heavenly Father to stress that He Himself is also of heavenly origin. He then goes further to say that 'the Father is in Him and He is in the Father.' Pushing the Father image to promote male hierarchy sadly takes us far away from the true intention of God's Word. God is not a gendered being and so we must dismiss all arguments that attempt to make a connection from God's authority to male authority in the church.[70]

FINAL THOUGHTS

Sometimes a text seems very clear. When some read one of these "black and white" texts, they just point to it and tell others to read the very obvious self-evident statement. But whether it's "Give no sleep to your eyes, nor slumber to your eyelids," or "I can do all things through Him *(Christ)* who strengthens me," or "I do not allow a woman to teach or exercise authority over a man, but to remain quiet," literary context must always be considered. Context is the king.

Like Monk who sensed when things were off, we need to closely investigate texts that seem odd (those red flag moments). Sometimes the key is found in other places, but often the answers are found in literary context. As students of God's Word, we're under no obligation to follow the accepted narratives that seem contrary to what we may sense the Holy Spirit is telling us. This grave mistake of adhering to the accepted narrative resulted in Christians supporting slavery for over 1,800 years.

If we truly want to bring the depths into focus (in this case, beyond the "black and white"), we must explore the "broader scriptural canvas"[71] (layers of context) that will help us see beyond the trees of "black and white" passages like 1 Timothy 2:12. The forest simply tells us another story.

Chapter 5

The Problem of Literalistic Reading

OVER THE YEARS, I'VE read many books on biblical interpretation. One of my favorites is a 1997 book by Robert Stein titled, *A Basic Guide to Interpreting the Bible: Playing by the Rules*. I must not be alone in my assessment of the book's value, because a second edition was published in 2011. Each time I teach a class about literary forms (genres), I begin by reading the following quote from Stein:

> Think for a moment of a European soccer fan attending his first (American) football and basketball games. In football the offensive and defensive players can use their hands to push their opponents. In basketball and soccer they cannot. In basketball players cannot kick the ball, but they can hold it with their hands. In soccer the reverse is true. In football everyone can hold the ball with his hands but only one person can kick it. In soccer everyone can kick the ball but only one person can hold it. Unless we understand the rules under which the game is played, what is taking place is bound to be confusing.[72]

Likewise, there are rules that must be understood when we read literary forms. Whether we think about it or not, we all intuitively know this. As proof, just think about a physical newspaper. First, consider the front section of the newspaper. It features city-wide headlines and important national news and, for the most part, is governed by one rule—it is serious news. Other sections, however, vary in their level of seriousness: entertainment, obituaries, lifestyle, comics, want ads, and sports.

To best illustrate how our interpretive skills shift from section to section, one only needs to compare the front headline news with the comics. When a person reads the headline news, they certainly do not expect to laugh. In fact, before they scan the page, they brace themselves for the potentially depressing news. Perhaps a three-alarm fire killed a family. Or perhaps a young teenager was gunned down in the street.

Unfortunately, front page news is not known for being the "feel good" area of the newspaper. Occasionally, of course, the front page may feature a story that brings happiness to the reader (e.g., the professional sports team just won the championship), but you'd be hard pressed to find a headline story that would make you laugh.

By comparison, a person doesn't pull out the comic section unless they want to laugh. The unwritten rule of the comic section is essentially that it is written and read with the goal of getting a good laugh.

When reading the newspaper, you never have to stop and remind yourself of the "rules," you just know them (with a possible exception being "editorials"[73]). One typically also make these shifts easily with literature and film. Take the 1997 blockbuster film *Titanic* as an example. Older viewers who saw the film at the theatre bought the ticket knowing good and well they were in for some serious and sobering content. They knew going in that many people died when the Titanic sunk in 1912. After all, it's a "disaster" film and the associated rules are pretty obvious.

I've always thought the old show M*A*S*H (1972 to 1983) was attractive to viewers because each episode would shift from comedy to drama so suddenly (what some have called "dramedy"). At one moment you found yourself laughing at the expense of Frank Burns, but before you knew it, the tragedy of war could have you tearing up—like when Colonel Blake was killed.

My point is that we know how to make these shifts in genre rather easily, even when it's a complicated shift within a mixed genre piece of work like M*A*S*H. But when it comes to reading the Bible, we are often unaware of the many literary forms present. Thus, we have a tendency to read most of the Bible like "serious news." And while there is certainly serious news, our Bible is very similar to a newspaper—and the various sections must be perceived and understood accordingly.

LITERAL READING

In the previous chapter, I stated how one can't "just read a text" and assume full understanding. I defined this approach as "black and white" reading, a method that ignores things such as backgrounds (chapter 3) and literary context (chapter 4). Here, the stress is that black and white reading also ignores the literary form of the passage.

The problem of black and white reading often lies in the "confusion over what it means to read literally."[74] Kevin Vanhoozer makes a distinction between "literal" and "literalistic." Vanhoozer explains that the "literal sense is a function of the author's communicative intent."[75] By contrast, a literalistic interpretation ignores the literary form. In other words, the faulty reading method I described above (what many refer to as reading the text in a literal way) is what Vanhoozer calls literalistic. Thus, we are correct to say that we should read the Bible in a literal manner, but only if we understand that the word "literal" takes into account the literary form that the author employed.

The problem lies in the fact that many believe they should read the Bible in a literalistic fashion. We might call this "taking the text at face value," or perhaps that "the text means exactly what it says." The intriguing thing about this faulty belief is that most of these same people can easily identify figurative speech, thus voiding their belief that the Bible must be read in this manner all the time. For example, most people understand David's poetic speech when he says he lifts his eyes to the hills because that's where his help comes from. We don't picture or believe God is actually, physically coming down the hill to help David.

Still, many Christians read the vast majority of Scripture in this faulty literalistic manner. Consider Colossians 1:19 as it says, "For it was the Father's good pleasure for all the fullness to dwell in Him."

This passage about the Christ is what I would call "serious headline news." We correctly take this at face value, as the literal meaning is exactly what the text says. The problem is that some read most of the Bible in this manner. I call this "flatlining."

Flatlining has a bit of a double meaning to me. First, it's like we read everything on the same flat plain (the "serious news" plain) with no changes or bumps along the way, when the reality is that a journey through the Bible is like taking the scenic route on a pathway with many types of terrain because it is full of various literary forms to explore. And second, it reminds me of a heart monitor that flatlines. The ominous sound of the monitor informs us that a heart has stopped, and life has left the body. When we read the Bible in only "serious headline news" manner, we can zap the life right out of the text. As a result, literary forms such as metaphor die at the doorstep of literalistic reading.

If we are to actually read the Bible with a literal approach, we must avoid flatlining. Instead, we must be keenly aware of the various literary forms used throughout Scripture.

LITERARY FORMS (GENRES)

These days, it seems that people are open to Jesus, but they're not generally thrilled about the Bible. Many think it is just an old boring book full of myths and useless religion. Furthermore, personal opinion is regarded much more highly than anything espoused in the Bible. The result is that fewer and fewer people seem to be reading God's Word, and that's a shame.

The Bible is anything but boring! But perhaps we have presented it in a boring way by not recognizing and helping others to see that it is bursting with a variety of literary forms. Consider the nine[76] primary genres in the Bible:

- Old Testament—narrative, law, poetry, prophecy, and wisdom literature

- New Testament—gospel, acts, letters, revelation[77]

And not to be forgotten are the many "sub-genres" that appear, such as: parable, rhetorical questions, irony, sarcasm, phenomenological language,[78] anthropomorphic language,[79] metaphor, simile, litotes (understatement), overstatement, and hyperbole.

As a collection of such a variety of literary forms, the Bible offers something for every taste. If reading law isn't your cup of tea, no worries because other literary forms are on the horizon. Do you love a good story? If so, you just hit the jackpot because about 40 percent of the Old Testament is made up of narrative. If you like poetry, you'll be happy to know that about 33 percent of the Old Testament is poetry.

In the New Testament, about 33 percent of Jesus' teachings in the synoptics[80] are comprised of parables, a genre that Jesus clearly loved. And if you like reading letters, it's nice to know that about 35 percent of the New Testament is made up of this literary form.

Awareness of the various literary forms is the first step to bringing the depths of the text into focus. The second is learning the "rules" attached to each genre. Describing all of the rules is simply beyond the scope of this book, and besides there are many great books[81] devoted to genre. In the following section, I'll demonstrate the importance of grasping the genre of the passage at hand.

THE NECESSITY OF GENRE IDENTIFICATION

I've been to some areas in both Mexico and Guatemala where people don't see the necessity of driving with the aid of traffic signs. To say the least, it's a nerve-racking experience I'm glad to have survived. It's always a relief to get home and encounter traffic signs/lights that provide clear driving instruction. Those simple colors of red, yellow, and green offer definitive guidance. If only the Bible were so clear.

The Bible may not flash lights at us to provide literary awareness, but thankfully many genres have clues that help us identify the form at hand. In the following, I'll provide four examples (two from the Old Testament and two from the New Testament) that will stress the importance of identifying the literary form. I'll also show how the signs of the literary form alert us to its presence.

Psalms

The Psalms are a beloved collection that contains a large section of the poetry found in the Old Testament. Poetry tugs at our emotions with figurative speech and a wide array of imagery. Just listen to David's opening words in Psalm 144:1–2:

> Blessed be the lord, my rock,
> Who trains my hands for war,
> And my fingers for battle;
> My lovingkindness and my fortress,
> My stronghold and my deliverer,
> My shield and He in whom I take refuge,
> Who subdues my people under me.

The imagery of this Psalm is a strong indicator that the reader has now entered the world of poetry. Granted, imagery is present throughout the Bible, but it is a staple feature found in poetry. Furthermore, stockpiled imagery is a hallmark of poetry. These two verses alone invite the reader to contemplate how the lord is a "rock," a "fortress," a "stronghold," a "deliverer," and a "shield."

While poetry is the primary literary form at hand (the umbrella if you will), it's also imperative to understand that there are various types of psalms. Besides the praise psalms we're mostly familiar with, some other types are laments, royal, and wisdom psalms. In other words, all psalms are not created equal. Thus, understanding that a psalm is poetry is one thing, but recognizing the specific type is also crucial.

My favorite psalms are lament psalms. Generally speaking, lament psalms can be found in the first half of the book of Psalms (1–75). In total, there are about sixty laments. I call laments "venting psalms" because that's exactly what you see the writers do in these.

I like the laments because the psalmists express what's really on their minds. They show authenticity, and by being transparent they verify to us that it's fine to express our true feelings to God who, after all, knows them anyway. I love how Craigie described them when he said, "They are real and natural reactions to the experience of evil and pain, and though the sentiments are in themselves evil, they are a part of the life of the soul which is bared before God in worship and prayer."[82]

Laments have distinctive characteristics that make them easy to identify. Though not all laments contain every one of the following, here are some defining features:

1. Address to God (invocation)

2. Complaints (description of distress)

3. Plea for God's help

4. Curse on enemies

5. Confession of sin *or* an assertion of innocence

6. Statement of confidence in God (or in his response)

7. Vow of praise for deliverance (hymn or blessing)

Psalm 79 is one lament that does contain all of the above features.

Essentially, in a lament the psalmist does a lot of complaining about life and wonders why God hasn't come to the rescue and brought judgment upon the bad guys. Finally, after all the venting has ceased, the writer takes a deep breath and says, "Okay lord, I know I've sinned too. And yes, in spite of my venting, I trust you to be God."

I've said all of this to lead up to this point—if you go looking for an uplifting psalm and land in a lament psalm, you may be very disappointed (unless you understand the differences). For example, let's compare the two psalms I've mentioned. For the most part, one walks away from Psalm 144 "feeling good." It is a royal psalm (with some praise features) where prayer is given to the lord who blesses and rescues his people. By contrast, the bulk of Psalm 79 feels like a "life-stinks" psalm that eventually concludes with the writer regaining his composure and simply trusting in God despite his woes.

Psalm 22:1–2 says,

"My God, my God, why have you forsaken me?
Far from my deliverance are the words of my groaning.
O my God, I cry by day, but You do not answer'
And by night, but I have no rest."

This is the beginning of a lament psalm written by David. It continues in verses 6–8, with David bemoaning the fact that people snicker at him as he trusts in a God who has not yet delivered him.

Now, let's consider a few composite characters I've created to illustrate the issue at hand. One I've named Bill has no awareness of the various types of psalms (the different genres). And let's also say that Bill has been going through some difficult times in his life (e.g., has cancer and now has lost his job, too). If Bill goes to the Psalms looking for a "feel good" psalm that extols the greatness of God but lands in Psalm 22, he may walk away feeling worse than before.

Bill was looking for one thing but got quite another—a psalmist confirming how much life can stink. Odds are, Bill won't even finish reading this psalm and will attempt to find another that makes sense to him. He missed the richness found in Psalm 22, but hopefully found another passage in Scripture that helped him.

Sue, however, is aware of lament psalms. She is also going through very difficult times. Furthermore, Sue is tired of her Christian friends giving the same pat answers to the trials that life has thrown her way. This frustration is, at least in part, birthed out of the fact that her friends have never experienced serious life challenges.

Sue begins reading Psalm 22 and has quite a different reaction to the text than Bill did. For the first time in a quite a while, Sue feels like she is listening to someone who understands the pain she is experiencing. She is comforted in knowing that if David can vent to God and express the same frustrations and doubts she feels, then she can also do the same. As she reads verse 10 ("You have been my God from my mother's womb") she begins to cry. After a pause, she keeps reading and comes to verse 19 which says, "But You, O lord, be not far off; O You my help, hasten to my assistance."

Psalm 22 was just the thing that Sue needed to read. She no longer feels alone in her struggle and is invigorated in her faith in God—such is the power of a good lament. As one can see, identification of the genre enables the Holy Spirit to use the power of God's Word to speak to the reader.

Proverbs

Unfortunately, our tendency towards "flatlining" is often seen when reading Proverbs. For example, people sometimes fail to distinguish the difference between a proverb and a letter like Romans which often provides propositional truths, what I've previously referred to as "serious headline news." Thus, it's important that readers understand the rules associated with wisdom literature (Proverbs, Ecclesiastes, Job, and perhaps Song of Solomon).

In Fee and Stuart's classic book, *How to Read the Bible for All It's Worth*, they describe Proverbs by saying they provide "rules and regulations people can use to help themselves live responsible, successful lives."[83] They even say that they might be called "old fashion basic values." Ewert echoes popular thought when he says, "Proverbs teach not absolute but probable truths. They offer general principles for successful living and do not spell out exceptions."[84]

The "general principles" of wisdom literature are quite different from the absolute truths we often read in the New Testament (e.g., "But while we were still helpless, at the right time Christ died for the ungodly"—Rom 5:6). But because literary forms are often ignored, Bible readers often make no distinction between the two.

A classic example is Proverbs 22:6 which says, "Train a child in the way he should go, even when he is old he will not turn from it." Regrettably, this great piece of instruction has frequently been turned into what I call "refrigerator theology"—a popular Bible verse that ends up being plastered to the front of the refrigerator, only to be incorrectly applied by all who "claim it in faith."

You've probably seen the following scenario. Mom has a child that is not living for Jesus, so Mom clings to this verse. "Remember," she says, "God's Word will not return void. I trained up my child in the ways of the lord. He will turn back to Jesus." Unfortunately, there are some major problems here, so many that I will carefully list them one by one.

1. This is wisdom literature. So, we must remember that this is not an iron-clad promise. Again, these are general principles that, if followed, will likely be true.

2. It's noticeable that God is not mentioned in this verse.

3. This verse says nothing about "returning" to God. The verse implies that the trained habits taught to a child will continue into adulthood. For example, if you train a child to be respectful of others, odds are the child will grow up as a respectful person. We may also conclude that

if a person trains up a child to love and serve God, it is likely that the child will continue to do so.

4. If it were an iron-clad promise about following after God, I would want to ask how long the child needs to be trained before the absolute promise kicks in.

5. If this were an iron-clad promise, I would want to also ask about the training. What if one parent teaches the child about God but the other does not, or even teaches contrary to God's laws?

6. Since wisdom literature dictates that these principles are generally true, the implication is that they are not always true. Thus, when the "promise that was claimed" does not materialize, the person of prayer could face a faith crisis, wondering if the Word of God is actually true. A simple lesson of wisdom literature would prevent the crisis.

7. Claiming such a "promise" can bring unnecessary guilt upon the parents of the "lost" child. They are now left to wonder what they did wrong.

8. If people have free will, then how could the "promise" be an absolute guarantee? One would have to take a strict Calvinist[85] position to believe in the "promise." Furthermore, teaching a strict promise/guarantee to the teenager may be seen as an implicit attempt to stifle a person's desire for individuality. This is the very thing that could incite them to rebel against their parents' desires.

9. People who misunderstand the genre of wisdom literature sometimes take a verse like this and judge others as being bad parents. In fact, they may begin to wonder if their so-called "Christian" friends are so in name only. After all, if they were 24/7 Christians, then their children would surely be living for Jesus.

10. I'm left to wonder if King David trained up his son Absalom in the way he should go. While we have little insight into the parenting skills of David, we know he was a man after God's heart (1 Sam 13:14). If this verse were an iron-clad promise, then one would have to conclude that David was a poor parent who did not pass on his love for God to his children.

11. Years ago, one of my students pointed out that God trained up Adam and Eve. Of course, they were not children, so perhaps he gets a free pass. Still, the thought bears some contemplation.

These eleven points show the many problems and/or implications of misinterpreting a text. We would be wise to heed Carson's words when he says, "A proverb is neither a promise nor case law. If it is treated that way, it may prove immensely discouraging to some believers when things do not seem to work out as the 'promise' seems to suggest."[86]

To support the rules of wisdom literature, Carson also asks us to consider the following proverbs that are located together:

- 26:4 says, "Do not answer a fool according to his folly, or you will be like him yourself."

- 26:5 says, "Answer a fool according to his folly, or he will be wise in his own eyes."

> A thoughtful reader will have to ask when it is best to follow one verse or the other . . . In other words, proverbs often demand meditation, subtle reflection of the circumstances under which the proverb applies, recognition that the proverb provides us with God-given wisdom on how to live under the fear of God, rather than simplistic univocal promises or the like.[87]

Life's complexities often leave us grasping for trusted answers. Through wisdom literature, God provides some help to us as we navigate the rough waters. We must simply remember the rules of the genre so that the Scriptures reach their intended result.

Hyperbole and Overstatement

If you've seen some "Jesus movies," you know that our lord is often depicted as a pretty serious guy. Likewise, portrayed as a man of sorrows, Jesus never smiles in historical art. It's unfortunate that we're often left with the impression that having a good time, laughing, or even smiling isn't really on Jesus' agenda.

If you need a quick cure for this problematic image of Jesus, here are three things you can do. First, get online and search for the picture of the "Laughing Jesus."[88] It was painted in 1973 by Willis Wheatley and has gained such popularity that many have copied it. Years ago, I used this image in a sermon. I still remember one guy telling me how much this ministered to him. He simply had never envisioned Jesus laughing.

Second, watch the 1993 movie *Matthew*.[89] In this film, Bruce Marchiano portrays Jesus in a refreshing manner. For example, he has a good time playing with the children. But one of my favorite parts occurs when Jesus delivers the Sermon on the Mount. As Jesus teaches the audience not to judge others (Matt 7:3–5), he picks up a large walking stick and laughs at the absurd image of the log in the eye. The crowd joins in the laughter.

Marchiano does a marvelous job of helping us correct our image of Jesus as being a boring overly stoic figure.

And finally, to help clarify your image of Jesus, I'd suggest reading the Gospels with a goal of picturing Jesus doing what is being described. As you get a broader image of Jesus, you'll come to see he used a variety of literary forms or techniques in his teaching. It is helpful to understand these techniques. In fact, the example just cited from Matthew 7 (the log in the eye) is what we call "hyperbole." Hyperbole is deliberate exaggeration. It was one of Jesus' favorite techniques[90] he used to gain the attention of the audience.

In our culture, we often cite hyperbole as any form of exaggeration. Technically, however, hyperbole is gross exaggeration[91]—exaggerating to the point that you're describing something that can't be done. This differs from overstatement. Though overstatement is also exaggeration, it is still within the range of something that actually can be done. Jesus loved to use both hyperbole and overstatement.

When you read a passage that sounds odd, or even absurd, you want to stop and ask yourself, "Could this be exaggeration?" If it makes you raise an eyebrow, there's a good chance Jesus is using one of these figures of speech. Beyond utilizing humor through exaggeration, Jesus clearly loved these figures of speech because of two other effects they can have.

First, exaggeration is memorable. I still vividly remember what happened in the top of the ninth inning in Game 5 of the 2005 National League Championship Series (NLCS). The Houston Astros were up by a score of four to two on the St. Louis Cardinals and had their closer, Brad Lidge, on the mound. At the time, Lidge was as close to unhittable as any pitcher could wish to be. But with two outs (one out away from reaching the World Series) and two runners on base, Albert Pujols launched a mammoth home run into left field that left the Astros' crowd in stunned silence.

The loss would send the Astros back to St. Louis for Game 6. To ease the tension on the flight, Astros catcher Brad Ausmus, had a little fun. "Ausmus dropped off a script for the pilot, who told the Astros that the airplane had reached cruising altitude and that, if they looked outside for the next three miles, they might see Pujols's home run ball. Everyone, including Lidge, thought it was hilarious."[92] Not only do I remember watching Pujols' classic shot, but I still remember the message Ausmus had the pilot deliver. That's the power of hyperbole.

Beyond being memorable, a good hyperbolic statement can also make the listener stop and think. Deep contemplation was surely Jesus' primary goal and it should be noted that even humorous hyperbole (e.g., the log in the eye) provokes contemplation.

Matthew 8:18–22 provides us with a great example of Jesus using both hyperbole and overstatement. It says,

> 18 Now when Jesus saw a crowd around Him, He gave orders to depart to the other side *of the sea.* 19 Then a scribe came and said to Him, 'Teacher, I will follow You wherever You go.' 20 Jesus said to him, 'The foxes have holes and the birds of the air *have* nests, but the Son of Man has nowhere to lay His head.' 21 Another of the disciples said to Him, 'Lord, permit me first to go and bury my father.' 22 But Jesus said to him, 'Follow Me, and allow the dead to bury their own dead.'

Verse 20 is clearly overstatement, as Jesus could simply lay his head down on the very spot where he is standing. Now, Jesus could have said, "I'm always on the move and sleeping arrangements aren't typically comfortable." But instead, he used overstatement. The figurative speech demands that you stop and process the statement. Jesus is not only addressing the issue of comfort, but he is also speaking to the fact that the unknown lies ahead. In other words, following after Jesus demands serious commitment. Even the birds have a routine of predictability in their lives (they have nests) but following after Jesus is anything but predictable. In essence, Jesus is asking, "Are you sure you want to follow me?"

Verse 22 is even more memorable, probably because it is hyperbole.[93] It's an absurd image. The dead simply can't bury the dead! The statement causes a great deal of reflection, which etches it deep into our memory banks. Jesus is stressing the urgency of following him right now, no matter how urgent the call to some other activity may appear. It would seem that Jesus is saying, "Let those who have no interest in the things of God (the spiritually dead) attend to the activities of the day (like burying the physically dead). Those who love God need to attend to what is most important. And nothing could be more important than following me."

Like verse 20, Jesus could have just stated verse 22 in a straightforward manner. He could have replied, "Let someone else bury your father. You need to follow me." Instead, Jesus gave the disciple much more—a statement about how true life can only be found in him.

Because Jesus utilized hyperbole so much, it's only appropriate to include another classic example (briefly mentioned in chapter 2). After Jesus' exchange with the Rich Young Ruler (Matt 19:16–22), he said the following to his disciples,

> 23 . . . 'Truly I say to you, it is hard for a rich man to enter the kingdom of heaven. 24 Again I say to you, it is easier for a camel to go through the eye of a needle, than for a rich man to enter

the kingdom of God.' 25 When the disciples heard *this*, they were very astonished and said, 'Then who can be saved?' 26 And looking at *them* Jesus said to them, 'With people this is impossible, but with God all things are possible.'

When speaking of verse 24, it's not uncommon to hear a teacher say something about there being a small gate in Jerusalem. We're sometimes told that if the rider dismounts the camel he can get through the small gate. The camel, however, will have to wait until the main gate is opened. A variation of this tells that if the camel's load is removed, it can barely get through this narrow gate.

In an attempt to explain this illogical statement of Jesus, they strove to find a key in a cultural background. The problem, however, is that no such gate existed in Jesus' day and the idea is based on a gate from the medieval period.[94] Bruce called this popular notion a "charming explanation . . . of [a] relatively recent date"[95] that is unsupported by evidence.

Charming (and convenient) as it may be to tie the explanation to an unrelated time period, it's more accurate to say Jesus is simply going back to the well of hyperbole. The absurdity of a camel fitting through the eye of a needle is obvious. Once again, Jesus wants his disciples to stop and contemplate the image and its application to the riches people accumulate. It draws to mind Jesus' words from the Sermon on the Mount, "You cannot serve God and wealth" (Matt 6:24b).

My wife Lisa says:

> What strikes me here (with this whole discussion) is that not recognizing hyperbole and seeking to instead find a plausible explanation (with the mismatched cultural background) actually takes away from Jesus' point. He is saying, 'The rich being able to enter heaven is actually that ludicrous, and in fact impossible. But don't worry, God makes the impossible possible.' By attributing the explanation to the hole in the wall image, we've actually made it appear the rich man can manage to squeak his way in on his own, without God.[96]

Jesus loved figurative speech and it's critical that it is properly identified. Misreading overstatements like, "If your right eye makes you stumble, tear it out" (Matt 5:29a) and "If your right hand makes you stumble, cut it off" (Matt 5:30a) could prove disastrous. Such literalistic interpretations could not only leave the obedient Christian maimed, they also fail to show the depths that Jesus loved to communicate.

Acts

It's not unusual to hear a Christian say something like, "At our church, we strive to be like the New Testament Church of the Bible." My first thought is always, "Which church?" While I know the person usually means the early church in the book of Acts, it's simply confusing to understand exactly what this statement means.

The word "church" isn't used until Acts 5:11 and describes the church at Jerusalem. By chapter 8, the church is being persecuted and "scattered throughout the regions of Judea and Samaria" (8:1). As we continue in Acts, we read of an expanding church that establishes local churches all over the place (Philippi—Acts 16, Thessalonica—Acts 17, Corinth—Acts 18, Ephesus—Acts 19, etc.).

In several different settings I've been exposed to, when people use the "we want to be like the NT church" phrase, they are referring specifically to the church as established in Acts 2. While the word "church" is not mentioned in that chapter, passages like Acts 2:41 use the word "added" ("added about three thousand souls") and beg the question, "Added to what?" We may rightfully conclude that they were added to the church.

At the heart of the assertion that some churches strive to be like the true New Testament church is the concept that the "original" church of Acts 2 is the ideal. While this is a commendable idea, it's simply impossible to separate the church in its origins from the church of its evolution. Life creates change and each chapter that follows Acts 2 shows the continual growth of the church from its infancy and its progression in different geographical and cultural contexts.

But for sake of argument, let's consider what it would mean (or how it would play out) if the church of Acts 2 is to be held as God's model for us. After Peter preaches the resurrected Christ, we're told, "So, then, those who had received his word were baptized, and that day were added about three thousand souls" (2:41). But listen to what follows,

> 42 They were continually devoting themselves to the apostles' teaching and to fellowship, to the breaking of bread and to prayer. 43 Everyone kept feeling a sense of awe; and many wonders and signs were taking place through the apostles. 44 And all those who had believed were together and had all things in common; 45 and they *began* selling their property and possessions and were sharing them with all, as anyone might have need. 46 Day by day continuing with one mind in the temple, and breaking bread from house to house, they were taking their meals together with gladness and sincerity of heart, 47 praising

God and having favor with all the people. And the Lord was adding to their number day by day those who were being saved.

As one can see, a close reading raises some questions and probable problems for many of us. Consider the following:

- Are we giving ourselves to "continual" devotion to Bible study, fellowship with other Christians, breaking of bread, and prayer?

- Does your church display "many wonders and signs?"

- Do we have "all things in common?" Do we sell our possessions to share our resources with brothers and sisters in need?

- Do we "day by day" share meals together in each other's homes?

After contemplating these questions, it's difficult to ignore the fact that most contemporary churches are void of wonders and signs. It's even more difficult to ignore the lifestyle choices we make which are in direct opposition to the values of the Acts 2 church. The challenge of "continual devotion" conflicts with sports leagues and family time, few people want to open their homes to others for even a simple dinner, and even fewer are interested in selling their possessions in order to share their wealth with others. We're left to ask, "Is there a single church today which actually emulates the church of Acts 2?"

The Acts 2 question, as interesting or convicting as it may be, is the wrong question. It serves, however, to illustrate a common problem we have in interpreting the narratives (the stories) in Acts. Akin to the flatlining problem discussed in our reading of Proverbs, is that people often read Acts and assume that the details speak to universal truths or patterns that should be followed. And this is where interpretation gets most difficult because, as Duvall and Hays explain, Acts is both story and theological history.[97] In other words, part of Acts is simply historical narrative (a recounting of the stories of God's people as they learn to follow him), while other parts are teaching deep truths.

The difficulty is in determining when a text is descriptive or prescriptive. Descriptive can be understood as *"what happened,"* whereas prescriptive is what *"must happen* in the ongoing church."[98] The "what must happen" portions are often referred to as "normative truths."

As you read the following passages from Acts, think about whether you and/or your church leaders view the various passages as descriptive or prescriptive:

- When choosing someone to take Judas' place, the disciples "drew lots" (1:26). Should we draw lots to make important decisions?

- "And they were all filled with the Holy Spirit and began to speak with other tongues" (2:4). Is speaking in tongues always the result of being filled by the Holy Spirit?

- "Peter said to them, 'Repent, and each of you be baptized in the name of Jesus Christ for the forgiveness of your sins, and you will receive the Holy Spirit'" (2:38). Should we baptize infants who have not repented of their sins?

- "And when they had prayed, the place where they had gathered together was shaken" (4:31). Should corporate prayer result in the miraculous?

- The church leaders at Antioch "fasted and prayed and laid their hands" on Paul and Barnabas before sending them out into ministry (13:1–3). Should fasting, prayer, and the laying on of hands always precede the commissioning of leaders?

- After Lydia's conversion, "she and her household had been baptized" (16:15). When an adult leader in the family is converted, should this person require baptism of the entire family?

- On the first day of the week, they "gathered together to break bread" (20:7). Are we required to take communion every week?

- A viper bit Paul and yet he "suffered no harm" (28:3–5). Should Christians be unconcerned about dangers?

When reading verses such as these, what becomes apparent is our interpretation is often influenced by our church background and various presuppositions. It's probably safe to say the vast majority of Christians view 1:26 and 28:3–5 as descriptive. Whether the remaining passages are descriptive or prescriptive, however, is debated among various church groups.

To ascertain what is descriptive or prescriptive in Acts, some important rules should be kept in mind. Duvall and Hays provide five guidelines:[99]

1. Look for what Luke intended to communicate to his readers

2. Look for positive and negative examples in the characters of the story

3. Read individual passages in light of the overall story of Acts and the NT

4. Look to other parts of Acts to clarify what is normative

5. Look for repeated patterns and themes

While each guideline is certainly important, perhaps the most important rule to keep in mind is number three. The study of New Testament teaching as a whole helps us recognize the normative teachings of Acts. This serves as a reminder that there are no short cuts to sound interpretation.

While looking to the whole New Testament is most helpful, even a brief consideration of guideline four, "look to other parts of Acts to clarify what is normative" is beneficial. As an example, the authors of *Introduction to Biblical Interpretation* show the varying models of church government described in Acts. They state the following:

1. 6:1–6—the entire congregation chose the apostle's helpers

2. 13:1–3—a select group of church leaders chose Barnabas and Saul for their missionary ministry

3. 20:17–38—Paul resembles a bishop who convenes all the Ephesian elders for instruction[100]

It's clear no single passage in this list can represent normal expectation for the contemporary church. This serves as a great example of how understanding the whole of Acts is critical.

While interpreting some literary forms is a skill easily acquired (e.g., lament psalms), closer study is required when properly discerning God's intention in Acts. While it's fairly simple to identify the overall literary form of Acts as narrative, healthy interpretation doesn't come quite that easily. Acts is truly a book that requires close reading and careful analysis.

FINAL THOUGHTS

When reading the Bible, we must remember it is full of various literary forms, and it is the many genres that help bring God's Word to life. One might think of the difference between watching a black and white film verses a colorized version, or perhaps loving the many colors in a rainbow.

I tend to think walking into an ice cream shop is a better illustration. There are many great flavors of ice cream to choose from, and from visit to visit you may eventually try them all. That's exactly how the numerous genres function for a reader of the Bible. We only need to learn the "rules" in order to fully understand and enjoy each literary form. Once the rules are understood, we can sample each scoop with great delight.

Chapter 6

The Problem of Application

I'VE BEEN INVOLVED IN sports my entire life. When I look back, I'm surprised at how many hats I've worn: player, official, writer, clock manager, athletics director, and coach. Like thousands of dads, I've coached kids at a lot of different levels (from t-ball to college, and everything in between).

As a coach, I always kept two things in the forefront of my mind, First, I've always believed athletes are at their best when they're having fun. So, I always tried to keep it fun and remember that games are just games. Any super competitive person will tell you how difficult this can be at times, and that's precisely the reason you need to keep reminding yourself why you actually play—it's for the fun.

Second, the coach's job is to teach individuals, prepare the team, and ultimately put them in a position to win. Basketball coaches, for example, may not hit game-winning shots, but they do everything in their power to put their players in that position. Ultimately, coaches never win games, players do.

The coach-player relationship reminds me of the preacher-listener (or teacher-student) relationship. Like the coach who attempts to put his players in a position to win, so does the preacher/teacher. The text is explained but ultimately the player-listener has to make something happen; they have to put what they have learned into action. In all truth, a sermon that lacks response is about as effective as X's and O's on a white board that a player only glances at.

Application is the name of the game. God has never told us to hoard knowledge. But he most definitely commands us to "do"—to obey, to go,—and you can insert all of the verbs and phrases the Bible provides; it's a long list of actions. Stated another way, we are not to be "listeners of the Word," but rather "doers of the Word."

Bible college and seminary students are taught about exegesis (pulling out the meaning of the text), but they are seldom taught about application. We must all remember, application is the ultimate goal of exegesis, and exegesis that does not conclude with application is a waste of time. As Westphal says, "Exegesis provides the foundation, but only with application do the people of God gain a home in which to dwell."[101] I doubt God is impressed with Bible knowledge that never moves out of the mind and into the heart.

I love what I heard Dr. Freddy Clark (a local preacher) say one day in chapel at St. Louis Christian College. He said, "Application is moving from exegesis to execution." Not only do I like the alliteration, but it reminds me of Hannibal Smith (*The A-Team*), who always said, "I love it when a plan comes together." For the A-Team, it ultimately all came together during the execution phase of foiling the always predictable bad guys. The lesson to be learned is this—when we obey God, action results in victory.

Preparation will never, in and of itself, result in victory. Action must be taken and the enemy hates when Christians are moved to action. Satan will often lie to us and tell us we must study, and then study some more before ever taking any kind of action. In an effort to learn, for example, we must attend yet another conference or read another book. None of this bothers the enemy. What drives the enemy crazy is when we both prepare and are moved to action. Movement, application, is what builds up the kingdom of God. And, of course, it's in making application that we move beyond the text itself.

OBSERVATIONS

Over the years, I've seen the following arrangements describe how one eventually moves from reading the text toward application:

- Read—Comprehend—*Apply*
- Explore it—Explain it—*Apply it*
- What?—So what?—*Now what?*
- What is it?—What's it worth?—*How do I get it?*
- What does it say?—What does it mean?—*What should I do?*

These all show the importance of application. I find it interesting that all five examples are listed in groups of three. I'm not sure if this is coincidental, or if it's just the preacher "threes," but the visual communicates that application is worth at least one-third of the interpretive process.

Yet, some preachers spend the vast majority of their time in exposition, to the detriment of application. Unfortunately, when preachers use this methodology, they leave the impression that a good Bible study is all that is necessary. When people are trained to view the goal of the sermon as such, you may hear them leaving church commenting on how much they learned from the message, but not discussing how they were changed or what they plan to do as a result of that learning.

Other preachers, while greatly concerned about application, sometimes make the opposite mistake of short-changing the biblical text. These sermons can leave the impression that the Bible wasn't even needed, or at the very least was just used as a springboard to get to the topic at hand. Congregants leaving the church after this kind of message might be heard saying something like, "I loved those five suggestions for sound investing." But most likely, they won't be commenting on how they were surprised the Bible had so much to say on finances or anything else related to the text.

These two examples both expose broken approaches. The former never gets to application. And the latter doesn't ground people in biblical truth, instead, opting to give helpful advice loosely based in biblical principles.

Daniel Overdorf[102] explains the problem by describing the indicative-imperative (what is true and what must be done) pattern found in Scripture and observes how some preachers "focus only on the indicatives and neglect the imperatives." Other preachers, "neglect the indicatives and jump straight to the imperatives."

I've always liked Veerman's illustration of the pyramid.[103] This visual depicts exegesis (going up the pyramid) and application (going down the pyramid), with both aspects being worth 50 percent of the process. It presents a balanced approach of study.

Overdorf describes the philosophical concern that lies at the heart of the imbalance often seen in preaching.[104] Some, he says, think it is the responsibility of the Holy Spirit to help the listener make application. Others, however, think it is the preacher's responsibility. But as Overdorf says, "Effective sermon application requires the involvement of both the Holy Spirit and the preacher."[105]

While I do not wish to turn this chapter into something that is only for "preachers," it must be admitted that they certainly have to deal with this issue on a regular basis. Furthermore, many church goers probably model their own process for making application from the preachers and teachers they hear on a regular basis.

Beyond the fact that preachers vary on the importance they place on application is the fact that most struggle in understanding how to draw application in a responsible way. Again, ministers are trained in exegesis but receive little instruction in the application process.

The problem is described well in *Introduction to Biblical Interpretation* when it says,

> Despite the importance of application, few modern evangelical scholars have focused on this topic. In fact, most hermeneutics textbooks give it only brief coverage, and many major commentary series only mention application with passing remarks to help readers bridge the gap from the biblical world to the modern world. Perhaps many assume that sound application is more 'caught than taught.' This is probably true, but sound application often seems hard to find, much less catch![106]

The opening words to Webb's book on exploring cultural analysis echo this idea that application is "hard to find." He said, "I welcome my reader to the fascinating world of applying Scripture. Here we encounter the complexities and challenges of moving from words on a page to actually living out the text within our lives."[107]

This challenge, even frustration, is grounded in several issues. First, while hermeneutics is both a science and an art, application is mostly an art. It's an art because, as much as anything else, it requires both prayer and involvement from the Holy Spirit.

It must simply be admitted that mystery often surrounds application. This is illustrated in the fact that ten listeners of a sermon will say the Holy Spirit spoke to them in various ways and brought about very different points of application. It's always puzzling when a listener tells the preacher what he/she said on Sunday was exactly what they needed. The preacher kindly smiles and later confesses to never having said what the listener "heard." One might be inclined to think the listener needs to listen more closely, but who's to say that the Holy Spirit wasn't somehow involved? I certainly would not say the Holy Spirit helped them "mishear." But who are we to say that the Holy Spirit didn't work through the process? These are mysterious waters to navigate, and we may say that the Holy Spirit helps us get "beyond the message."

Another challenge to drawing application is the fact that there is a difference between understanding general guidelines for application and possessing a clear process (scientific method) for it. Certainly, many have provided general guidelines. But nobody has provided a definitive process. It's not for lack of effort,[108] it's simply because application is mostly art. As

Porter says, "the move from the original text of Scripture, with all of its time-bound character, to theological truths for life today is one of the most demanding intellectual tasks imaginable."[109]

This brings us to yet another issue: application often involves trying to discern if a text is "culturally bound" or "timeless/universal."[110] This is every bit as difficult as application itself, thus the problem.

And finally, adding further frustration, Mueller points out, "We not only identify the significance of texts differently, depending on whether they are biblical, church historical, or contemporary, we also understand texts differently, depending on the relationship between their context of understanding and our own."[111] In other words, our interpretations can influence the significance we give a text. Furthermore, if our interpretations vary, our applications are bound to vary as well.

The bottom line is that making good application is difficult, takes effort, is somewhat mysterious, and must include prayer. This explains, in part, why many preachers are good at explaining the text, but poor at making meaningful application.

While making confident and sound application is a challenge, some important progress has been made. In the upcoming sections we will explore some application models that have been presented. After a review of the models, I will share my thoughts on best practices by providing seven propositions for sound application. Because various authors have described the application process with varied terms, I have grouped models together that show similarity. Furthermore, to increase understanding, I thought it may be helpful to see a snapshot of the models before proceeding.

Application Models	
Principlizing/ Abstraction Ladder	Finding the timeless principle in the text and applying it to new situations.
Trajectory/ Redemptive-Spirit/ Developmental	The biblical message is a foundation of truth that, within new cultural contexts, may lead to more complete understanding.
Five-Act Hermeneutic/ Drama-of-Redemption	As transformed believers, we allow the Holy Spirit to speak new understandings of the text that impact our actions in a modern world.

PRINCIPLIZING/ABSTRACTION LADDER MODELS

A widely accepted method is what we may call *"principlizing."*[112] Kaiser Jr. said that to principlize, one needed to discover the "timeless truths" of the author and then apply them in the current situation.[113]

Many others follow this method and have built on this foundation.[114] For example, Kuhatschek described this process as (1) understanding the original situation, (2) finding the general principles, and (3) applying the general principles.[115] In other words, find the timeless principles that are transcultural.

The problem, of course, is how does a person responsibly establish the principles present in the text? Kuhatschek advised that three critical questions[116] should be asked. First, does the author state a general principle? Second, why was a specific command or instruction given? And third, does the broader context reveal a general principle?

McQuilken cited four sources of biblical principles.[117] There are, he said, (1) explicitly stated principles, (2) general principles derived from explicit declaration, (3) general principles derived from historical passages, and (4) general principles derived from passages that do not directly apply to contemporary life.

When formulating his visual pyramid, Veerman arrives at the principles by asking, (1) what is the message for all of humankind?, (2) what are the timeless truths?, and (3) what is the moral of the story?[118]

Listing five "criteria for formulating the theological principles,"[119] Duvall and Hays say that the principle should: (1) be reflected in the text, (2) should be timeless and not tied to a specific situation, (3) not be culturally bound, (4) correspond to the teaching of the rest of Scriptures, and (5) be relevant to both the biblical and the contemporary audience.

Haddon Robinson's *"abstraction ladder"*[120] is essentially the same concept as finding the principle, although he spoke of ascertaining two primary points of interest: what does the text teach about both God and about human depravity (human nature)?[121] Most helpful was Robinson's advice on distinguishing between various types of implications in the text, those implications being either necessary, probable, possible, improbable, or impossible. The types of implication provide a nice method to preventing serious error.

Others[122] have also chimed in to support principlizing. Clark,[123] however, pointed out three problems with the "principlizing" method. One problem is that our cultural biases can contaminate the principles we detect. Second, Clark believes that an emphasis on principles favors didactic texts.[124] Third, it is dangerous to take determined principles as being a "more accurate indication of God's will than its canonical expression."[125]

TRAJECTORY/REDEMPTIVE-SPIRIT/ DEVELOPMENTAL MODELS

"Principlizing," while certainly the most popular approach for making application, is not the only model. Longenecker described a *"developmental hermeneutic"*[126] in his 1984 book, *New Testament Social Ethics*. Foundational to this hermeneutic are four conclusions,[127] one which in part says, "The ethical statements of the New Testament are given not as detailed codes of conduct but as principles[128] or precepts which seek primarily to set a standard for the kind of life pleasing to God, to indicate the direction we ought to be moving."

Note the key phrase, "direction we ought to be moving." In discussing the developmental model, Longenecker says it, "speaks of both continuity with a foundational core and genuine growth in conceptualization and expression. It is a model that appeals by way of analogy to the relationship between a growing plant and its original seed."[129] Longenecker insightfully adds,

> Seed sometimes grows in spurts and in aberrant ways, and so, sadly, does love. So in theology, as in all of life, there is the need to develop healthy growth patterns, to be able to identify continuity as well as development, and to be conservative in our reaching back to our revelational base as well as creative in our moving forward to a fuller understanding and a better application.[130]

It seems the real distinction is that principlizing suggests we take the underlying principle (often not stated in the text) and apply it to now, while Longenecker pushes even further to say we need to determine how the principles (stated in the text) are meant to propel us toward changes for the future.[131] The following may help in understanding Longenecker's thought process, as he says,

> The New Testament . . . is not a textbook on systematic theology. It is a record of God's revelation and redemption in Jesus Christ and a record of the Church's initial attempts to understand and state what all that means. To be biblical is not to say only what the New Testament says, 'nothing more or less,' as some would claim. Rather, the biblical Christian realizes that

the Bible, history, and reason all come into play in constructing a Christian theology: the first as the touchstone for truth and as the pointer to the path that should be involved; the second as a record of how the Church has tread that path throughout the centuries, with attention to both the advances and the pitfalls; the third in determining where the history of theology has been in continuity with its revelational base and how Christian theology should be expressed today.[132]

Longenecker spends a majority of this small book using Galatians 3:28 as a case study for showing why development is necessary. Prior to the case study, he says the writers of the New Testament "began to work out the implication of . . . [the] gospel for the situations they encountered—not always, admittedly, as fully or as adequately as we might wish from our later perspectives, but appropriately for their day and pointing the way to a fuller understanding and more adequate application in later times."[133]

Fifteen years after completion of the aforementioned book, Longenecker wrote *New Wine into Fresh Wineskins*. Here, he discussed various models for an understanding of contextualization.[134] Among those, is the "translation model," a model that adapts principles to new situations (what we previously called "principlizing"). He cites three weaknesses,[135] and while all are perceptive, it seems most notable that this model "often treats Scriptures in a rather static fashion."

Longenecker opts, instead, for what he now calls the *"synergistic-developmental"* model. There are two fundamental realizations that are basic to this model. He says,

> (1) that an understanding of Scripture and an understanding of a particular culture can not come about simply from a static view of the phenomena but, rather, must be constructed with an appreciation that development has taken place in both sets of data; and (2) that relations between the gospel and any culture are synergistic—that is, they are meant by God to work together in order to produce a truly contextualized theology and lifestyle.[136]

He further clarifies, "The first realization highlights the need to study Scripture and its resultant traditions, on the one hand, and particular peoples and their cultures, on the other, in terms of their central concerns and their cultural variations."[137]

In describing his analogy of the seed in greater detail, Longenecker compares the synergistic-developmental model to the process of taking two seeds from one original plant and planting them in different locations. The resulting plants may differ in appearance because they were cultivated in different circumstances—different soils and climates, for example. Still, they will essentially bear the same fruit. What is significant in the long-term is how the two plants will cross-pollinate with native plants of their new surroundings and each will produce a unique hybrid. Again, however, Longenecker points out the "hybrid will produce fruit somewhat different, but still very much like the fruit of the original seed." Likewise, this is what we find when the seeds of the Gospel are planted "into various ideological contexts and diverse cultural situations, where the seeds come to maturity and cross-pollinate in the context of their respective receptor peoples and cultures." Those "new flowerings of Christianity," according to Longenecker, are found to be "faithful both to the apostolic faith of the NT and to the cultures and perspectives of those addressed."[138]

R. T. France spoke of "*trajectory*,"[139] his way of describing how we must place an issue in a complete canonical context and then ascertain its forward movement. He further states, some are "hermeneutically naïve, . . . mind-lessly quoting proof-texts without recognizing either that the horizon of the biblical writers is different from ours or that even within the pages of the Bible there is development and growth, so that not all biblical texts neces-sarily carry the same relevance to a later context."[140]

France says that application "moves us into an area of uncomfortable flexibility."[141] While every Christian can attest to the fact that trying to apply Scripture to our everyday lives often brings discomfort, France pushes even further. He speaks of how trajectory leads to new insights of application that may challenge us at our very core.

Following France's work, Webb offered what he called the "*redemptive-movement hermeneutic*."[142] He says this hermeneutic "investigates the big picture or meta-framework through which we look at Scripture."[143] Webb encourages us "to engage the redemptive spirit of the text in a way that moves the contemporary appropriation of the text beyond its original-application framing."[144] This is needed because there are times when "living out the Bible's literal words in our modern context fails to fulfill its redemp-tive spirit."[145]

Webb maintains that a redemptive lens "encourages movement be-yond the original application of the text in the ancient world," a contrast to static appropriations of Scripture where the "underlying spirit" of the text is minimized.[146] Because Webb's approach "looks at a component of mean-ing *within* the biblical text and canon," he wonders if some would prefer to label his approach a "progressive" or "developmental" or "trajectory" hermeneutic.[147]

Believing that "principlizing a text up the abstraction ladder is simply not far enough,"[148] Webb asserts that the "redemptive spirit underlying a text should be distinguished from what is commonly known as the principle underlying a text."[149]

Webb readily admits that "finding the underlying spirit of a text is a delicate matter."[150] Nevertheless, the "ultimate ethic is reflected in the spirit of the biblical text"[151] and should be sought, because a static approach "fails to breathe into the new setting a measure of the empowering life force that made the text redemptive in its own day."[152]

While Webb offers eighteen criteria for exploring cultural analysis, I will briefly mention only three of them. His first criterion, "preliminary movement," is defined as the biblical author pushing "society as far as it could go at that time without creating more damage than good; however, it can and should ultimately go further."[153]

In his second criterion, Webb describes "seed ideas," seeds not fully grown in Scripture that encourage further movement. Webb elaborates, "Texts with seed ideas would probably have moved the original audience only in a limited fashion."[154] While these biblical texts may not have pushed societal action as immediately as the "preliminary movement" texts, by subtly planting thoughts and ideas into the minds and hearts of the readers they will bear fruits of change as they mature.

Webb's fourth criterion finds a text transcultural if it is based in the Fall or Curse.[155] I find this particularly important, as scholars often support their arguments with the claim that the principle they're espousing is "based on the Creation account." While I completely agree with the basic idea, many speak of Genesis 3 as if it is also God's ideal. Living out the curse, however, is clearly not God's ideal. While we still see effects of the curse, we must remember that Christ set in order a work of redemption.

Eight years after his noteworthy book, Webb presented his "redemptive-movement" model (with some clarification) in *Four Views on Moving Beyond the Bible to Theology*.[156] He begins by explaining what is meant by "moving beyond the Bible," and defines the phrase as moving beyond "concrete specificity," or "time-restricted elements," or pushing beyond "isolated or static" understanding of the Bible.[157] This is vital, as some critics have difficulty getting past the words "beyond the Bible." Others "do not want to venture beyond the Bible in any sense. Many would much rather stay with the concrete specificity of the biblical text because it offers a sense of safety."[158] This safety, however, can result in poor interpretation.

In explaining the "redemptive-movement" hermeneutic, Webb says,

> Scripture seems to give us an ethic that needs in some ways to be developed and worked out over time. It would appear that many biblical texts were written within a cultural framework

with limited or *incremental movement* toward an ultimate ethic. If so, then possibly 'movement meaning' within the text itself ought to tug at our heartstrings and beckon us to go further.[159]

Webb says, "The essence of the RM [redemptive-movement] model can be captured succinctly in three or four words: 'Movement is (crucial) meaning.' . . . Movement meaning [is] captured from reading the text in (1) its ancient *historical and social* context and (2) its *canonical* context, which yields a sense of the underlying spirit of the biblical text."[160]

Wishing to clarify any misinterpretation of his words, Webb is clear in that, "The 'redemptive movement' is an element of meaning within the actual words of the biblical text."[161] This is precisely why Webb states the importance of canonical context. To explain how one moves from the literal words of the text to considering a potential trajectory of teaching, Webb astutely observes, "Understanding the NT [New Testament] as final and definitive *revelation* does not automatically mean the NT contains the final *realization* of social ethics in all of its concrete particulars."[162] To help us understand this realization, Webb says,

> The idea of the RM hermeneutics is not that God himself has somehow 'moved' in his thinking or that Scripture is in any way less than God's Word. Rather, it means that God in a pastoral sense accommodates himself to meeting people and society where they are in their existing social ethic, and (from there) he gently moves them with incremental steps towards something better. Moving large, complex, and embedded social structures along an ethical continuum is by no means a simple matter. Incremental movement within Scripture reveals a God who is willing to live with the tensions between an absolute ethic in theory and the reality of guiding real people in practice toward a goal.[163]

In *Beyond the Bible*, I. Howard Marshall also discussed the "*developmental theory.*" Marshall says,

> What we have at work in the New Testament . . . is a combination of the apostolic deposit and Spirit-given insight. These two factors work together to detect error and to promote true development in Christian doctrine and practice. The combination of a doctrinal, christological criterion and a renewed mind enables believers to develop the implications of their faith and to come to fresh insights to deal with new knowledge and the danger of false belief. By these means believers were able to assess new

revelations by prophets and new teaching of other kinds, and
this led to fuller development of doctrine.[164]

As an example of how further development is necessary, Marshall
discusses how a Christian may respond to issues surrounding abortion,
euthanasia, or genetic engineering. "In such a situation there would be a
new expression of Christian theology that has to be tested specifically for
its Christian character in light of Scripture but that is on another level of
experience. Clearly, christological orthodoxy alone is inadequate as a test;
we would need, in this example, to explore the biblical understanding of
humanity."[165] In this latter statement, Marshall reminds us that canonical
study is imperative.

Democracy is stated as another example of going beyond Scripture.
Marshall maintains that, in spite of the fact that non-democratic forms of
government are the accepted norms found in Scripture, it's unlikely that a
Christian today would defend them.[166]

He also mentions the Council at Jerusalem that wrote Paul and instructed him to have the Gentile Christians "abstain from the things
sacrificed to idols and from blood and from things strangled and from for-
nication" (Acts 15:29). Marshall notes that Gentiles observed this decree for
some time, but it did not last. For example, Gentiles no longer follow the
decree about abstaining from meat that may have blood in it.[167]

Marshall reiterates the safeguard of canonical control when he says,
"The principle I am proposing . . . is this: we should take our guidance for
our continuing interpretation of Scripture and the development of theology
from what goes on in Scripture itself."[168] This is something he reiterates in
his closing statements that recap the seven[169] primary points he hopes to
establish.

Vanhoozer offered critique of Marshall's developmental theory by
suggesting a "*christological trajectory that employs canonical practice.*"[170] He
states that movement leading to the "wisdom of God summed up in Christ"
should not go beyond this point, "even when that something is associated
with the Spirit."[171] In discussing the canonical approach, he says, "Embedded in the canon are the patterns for correct speaking and thinking about
God, patterns of judging that represent nothing less than the substance of
'sound doctrine.'" Furthermore, he stresses that, "Expositors of Scripture . . .
must learn not simply to parse the verbs or to process the information, but
to render the same kind of judgments as those embedded in the canon in
new contexts and with different concepts."[172]

Vanhoozer elaborates,

Canonical practices are rule-governed forms of covenantal behavior that direct the seeing, judging, and acting of the believing community. We acquire canonical competence—a mind nurtured on the Christ-centered canon—when we learn how to make the same kind of judgments about God, the world, and ourselves as those embedded in Scripture.[173]

Vanhoozer believes his approach works within the redemptive trajectory approach, as it recognizes "there is movement within Scripture," but he insists on a christological focus that erects a "canonical fence around the gospel lest the gospel be taken captive by other ideological interests."[174] Vanhoozer's approach is certainly appealing. However, I wonder if it is too restrictive, as it may not allow for Marshall's concerns for contemporary issues that are beyond the imagination of the biblical writers.

FIVE-ACT HERMENEUTIC/
DRAMA-OF-REDEMPTION MODEL

N. T. Wright's work, *The Last Word*,[175] is worthy of mention. He reminds us that God's Word is "living, active, powerful and fruitful" (Isa 40:8; 55:11; Heb 4:12).[176] Wright says, "This should generate the hope that, through a fresh reading and teaching of Scripture, our present culture and all that goes with it will be addressed and challenged by new and God-given viewpoints."[177]

Wright stresses that to understand Scripture, we need some type of "overarching narrative" that will help us make sense of the texts.[178] He proposes a *five-act hermeneutic* which "involves knowing where we are within the overall drama and what is appropriate within each act. The acts are: creation, 'fall,' Israel, Jesus, and the church."[179]

With the New Testament being the foundational charter and first scene of the fifth act (the church), we take this standard and improvise the subsequent scenes. "Our task is to discover, through the Spirit and prayer, appropriate ways of improvising the script between the foundation events and charter, on the one hand, and the complete coming of the Kingdom on the other."[180] Wright is both careful and clear about what he means by "improvising." He says,

As all musicians know, improvisation does not at all mean a free-for-all where 'anything goes,' but precisely a disciplined and careful listening to all the other voices around us, and a constant attention to the themes, rhythms and harmonies of the complete performance so far, the performance which we are now called to continue. At the same time, of course, it invites us, while being fully obedient to the music so far, and fully attentive to the voices around us, to explore fresh expressions, provided they will eventually lead to that ultimate resolution which appears in the New Testament as the goal, the full and complete new creation which was gloriously anticipated in Jesus's resurrection. The music so far, the voices around us, and the ultimate multi-part harmony of God's new world: these, taken together, form the parameters for appropriate improvisation in the reading of scripture and the announcement and living out the gospel it contains.[181]

Wright issues a warning of sorts when he adds, "Any church, not least those that pride themselves on being 'biblical,' needs to be open to new understandings of the Bible itself."[182] He says that this is the "only way to avoid being blown this way or that by winds of fashion, or trapped in one's own partial readings and distorted traditions while imagining that they are a full and accurate account of 'what the Bible says.'"[183]

Vanhoozer suggests a *drama-of-redemption model*[184] which has some similarity to Wright's "five-act hermeneutic." He says he is "deploying a number of themes and concepts that will prove fruitful in our search for Christian understanding."[185] Vanhoozer sheds some light on his model when he says, "Theology involves not only theoretical but *theatrical* reasoning: *practical* reasoning about what to say and do in particular situations in light of the gospel of Jesus Christ."[186]

"What Christian readers of Scripture are ultimately trying to understand are not principles as much as the divine play described, implied, and projected by the script,"[187] says Vanhoozer. He adds, "In speaking of 'performing' the script, . . . I have in mind not reproducing the world behind the text or of recreating the scenes depicted in the text but rather of living in a way that conforms to the world as it is being transformed 'in Christ.'"[188]

In other words, the Christian should be moved to "action"[189] by the implied and projected script that aligns itself with Christ, and the canon[190] as a whole. We are to appropriate the message of the text as we are being transformed "by watching/hearing it properly, as a word about who this God is that we are trying to know and love."[191] This process involves discernment. I believe Vanhoozer's ensuing comment sums up his model well when he says,

We move beyond the script and become faithful performers of the world it implies by cultivating minds nurtured on the canon. The aim of the drama-of-redemption approach is to train and discipline the believer's mind, heart, and imagination to think, desire, see—and then *do*—reality as it is in Jesus Christ. Moving 'beyond' the sacred page involves more than applying it; it involves renewing and transforming the people's habits of seeing, thinking, and acting. Scripture is not merely a vehicle for conveying information. It is rather a medium of divine communicative action whose purpose is not only to inform but to transform: to nurture right vision, right attitudes, right actions.[192]

THOUGHTS ON THE VARIOUS APPLICATION MODELS

Since it is not my goal to present a complete history of the various application models[193] which have been offered, I will conclude here. It is beyond the scope of this book to critique each model, and besides, many have already offered assessments. A few words, however, seem appropriate.

First, having been in preaching ministry for twenty-five years, I can attest to the fact that sometimes the "principlizing" method works and, at other times, it fails miserably. I know some will disagree and say "principlizing" works for them, but my contention is that it fails when background study is necessary.[194]

When an interpreter considers backgrounds (e.g., historical, cultural, geographical) of utmost importance, it naturally leads to a more complete understanding of the text. While most interpreters will attest to the importance of understanding backgrounds, it is also clear that some are quick to dismiss them, instead favoring the "black and white" reading of the text. Unfortunately, the person who fails to actually embrace historical concerns is left with a text that is often misinterpreted.

When one allows critical backgrounds to influence the meaning of the text, a difficulty in application arises, as this layer of complexity makes establishing a principle much more daunting. This is why I say that sometimes "principlizing" doesn't work. It works when backgrounds are not critical to interpretation, but it fails when backgrounds impact understanding. Thus, the primary difference between those who embrace a "principlizing" method verses others who see some type of "trajectory" model ("development," "improvisation," or "transformation requiring discernment") lies in a person's willingness to see beyond the literal words of the text. This is clearly the strength of the latter methods surveyed.

This leads to my second point, the "trajectory" models must be taken seriously despite an understandable hesitancy to stray too far from what is explicitly written in the text. Most serious Bible students do want some sense of boundaries or controls on the interpretive process and recognize the potential of the interpreter imposing their own ideas onto the text.

However, these cautions must not be used to curtail any effort to see beyond the text.

It might be helpful to keep in mind that the same arguments could be made against interpretation in general, because no human is capable of complete objectivity. We all bring presuppositions to the text. Even when utilizing a strict hermeneutical approach, which takes much subjectivity out of the process, we are never guaranteed that the human interpreter will get it right. Still, does all this mean we should never try to interpret Scripture at all because we fear these potential pitfalls?

Fear can be paralyzing and that is not fitting for the Christian who is being transformed by the presence of the Holy Spirit. God's Word has an amazing depth that teaches beyond specific cultures. I concur with Webb when he states, "It is a trajectory or logical extension of the Bible's redemptive spirit that carries Christians to an ultimate ethic."[195] Within the guardrails of canonical expression, and by the aid of the Holy Spirit, we simply must bring the depths of the text into focus.

SEVEN PROPOSITIONS

Instead of attempting to formulate a strict process for sound application, I propose a series of guidelines that should be contemplated.

1. *The example of Jesus is always our starting point.*

Methodology that forgoes a study of Jesus simply falls short. The complexities surrounding sound application make it all the more imperative to understand how Jesus viewed the process. Reading through the gospels, a few things become clear.

First, *Jesus placed great emphasis on application.* At the very least, this informs us that we must also actively engage in making application. A mere glance at the Sermon on the Mount (Matt 5–7) demonstrates Jesus' concern. As Alvord said, "Jesus highly valued application and employed it liberally."[196] While Alvord speaks directly of the Sermon on the Mount, his words speak to a pattern we see in Jesus. It seems that almost anywhere we turn in the gospels, Jesus is giving new understanding of Old Testament teaching, or new application of both the Law and the cultural customs of the day.

A very quick survey of Matthew's gospel account resulted in the following observations. Matthew 5 features the six wrong sayings (the antitheses) where Jesus repeatedly says, "You have heard it was said . . . but I say." The applications Jesus draws can be seen in the following:

- 5:21–26   Murder with application of anger
- 5:27–30   Adultery with application of lust
- 5:31–32   Divorce with application of adultery
- 5:33–37   Vows with application of truthfulness
- 5:38–42   Revenge with application of charitability
- 5:43–47   Hate with application of love

Moving further into the book of Matthew, when Jesus is accused of being a Sabbath breaker (Matt 12:1–8, 9–14), he corrects the understanding of the Pharisees. Just a few verses later (Matt 12:46–50), he makes new applications in regard to what family is by saying all those who do the will of God are his true family. Then in Matthew 18:15–20, he quotes Deuteronomy 19:15 (two or three witnesses, see also Num 35:30; Deut 17:6) that was originally given in the context of law and repurposes it to apply to matters in the church.

Second, *Jesus used a complete canonical approach to interpretation, whereas, the religious leaders failed to see importance in the exceptions that would challenge their interpretations.* The Matthew 12:1–8 passage mentioned above tells of the disciples picking grain on the Sabbath, which the Pharisees note is unlawful (Exod 20:8–11). To correct their understanding, Jesus points to greater canonical context. He gives two examples, citing how David and his companions ate of the consecrated bread (1 Sam 21:1–6) and also how the priests in the temple continually break the Sabbath, yet are innocent.

In essence, the Pharisees were hung up on Exodus 20 (and its reiteration in Deut 5:12–15). It's difficult to blame them, as they viewed the Ten Commandments as being more significant than other passages. But Jesus disagreed with their view that the exceptions were insignificant and "lesser than" the Ten Commandments. He demonstrated that the whole of Scripture must always be considered.

Another example can be seen in the temptation of Jesus (Matt 4:1–11). In the second temptation (vv. 5–7), the devil takes Jesus to the pinnacle of the temple and quotes Psalm 91:11–12 saying, "If you are the Son of God, throw Yourself down; for it is written, 'He will command His angels concerning You' and 'On their hands they will bear You up, so that You will not strike Your foot against a stone.'"

Jesus replies by appealing to Deuteronomy 6:16. He says, "On the other hand, it is written, 'You shall not put the lord Your God to the test.'" By appealing to a second Old Testament passage, Jesus once again shows that it is a dangerous method to ignore the complete canonical message.

Third, *Jesus was concerned about the "spirit" of the text, something that surely shocked the teachers of his day*. As Jesus applied Old Testament Scripture in new ways, the religious leaders found him to be a liberal who grossly abused the sacred text. While the religious leaders may have interpreted the text properly to its original setting, they failed to grasp the "spirit" of the text, the greater understanding that lies beyond the text itself. Thus, they failed immensely at applying the text well.

Some, while acknowledging this truth, would suggest that how Jesus applied Scripture has little to do with how we may approach it. And while it's pretty obvious that we, in no way, can speak with the authority that Jesus did, it is a mistake to ignore what Jesus has taught us about both reading and applying the text.

It is our duty to treat the text as living and active, something that fluidly invades our lives and speaks to us in ways that should shape our lives. Jesus exhibited a new way of applying Old Testament text, moving us toward higher ideals. This should, at the very least, make us consider whether we ought also to do the same.

A prime example of how Jesus emphasized the spirit of the text is found in Matthew 19:3–9. Here, some Pharisees come to test Jesus by asking, "Is it lawful for a man to divorce his wife for any reason at all?" Jesus responds by quoting Genesis 2:24, then saying, "So they are no longer two, but one flesh. What therefore God has joined together, let no man separate." In reply, the Pharisees provide their own Scripture of choice (Deut 24:1) and ask, "Why then did Moses command to give her a certificate of divorce and send her away?"

Jesus' response is telling. He says, "Because of your hardness of heart Moses permitted you to divorce your wives, but from the beginning it has not been this way" (v. 8). In his answer, Jesus sees beyond the literal words of the text, piercing to the true spirit of the text. It should not be lost on us that in doing this, Jesus essentially *explores the cultural background* surrounding the decision of Moses.

Finally, we must observe how this conversation ends in verse 9. The leaders clearly think that if a man divorces a woman, he is free to remarry. Jesus sets right this error and informs them that a man who divorces his wife and remarries commits adultery (except in cases of immorality).

To see further examples of how Jesus viewed the spirit of the text as essential, we only need to return to the Sermon on the Mount. In the first "wrong saying" (Matt 5:21–26), for example, Jesus reveals the action of murder as beginning with thoughts and statements that belittle another (e.g., "you're a fool," "you're good for nothing," or "I'm angry because you won't see things my way, the right way"). Issues of superiority and self-reliance may cause one to think they have no use for another human being. This is the heart of the matter that can lead to murderous actions.

By emphasizing the spirit of the command, Jesus informs us that when we think we have no need for others, we are committing murderous thoughts that often result in murderous-like speech and action. While they may not result in the termination of life, they result in a corruption of self. Corrupt actions (sin) always make us accountable to the Judge.

Fourth, *Jesus' message about the fresh wineskins ("new wine must be poured into new wineskins"—Luke 5:37-38; cf. Matt 9:17; Mark 2:22) may speak to more than the fact that the gospel is not to be confined within the boundaries of Judaism. It may indicate that Jesus' followers are to be involved in contextualizing the gospel in new ways.*[197]

As Longenecker says, "If the message of the kingdom of God as focused in Jesus is to be communicated effectively, it must always be proclaimed and worked out in ways that are relevant to the worldview and culture of those being addressed."[198] Marshall agrees, and says, "To attempt to contain the gospel within the bounds of Judaism will only destroy both. But the saying goes further and makes a positive point: the gospel is radically new and must be allowed to express itself in its own way."[199]

Longenecker also notes a somewhat parallel statement of thought in Matthew 13:52. Verses 51–52 are a conclusion to a series of parables on the kingdom. Here, Jesus asks the disciples, "Have you understood all these things?" After they answer, "Yes," Jesus then says, "Therefore every scribe who has become a disciple of the kingdom of heaven is like a head of a household, who brings out of his treasure things new and old." Longenecker comments,

> Many features of this brief concluding parable are fairly easy to understand. The 'kingdom of heaven' is certainly the reign of God in people's lives, as proclaimed by, effected by, and fo-cused in Jesus. Likewise, the 'teacher of the law who has been instructed about the kingdom' is one who is committed to and instructed by Jesus—that is, a Christian teacher, not some Jew-ish scribe trained in the traditions of the Pharisees. It is also ob-vious that the parable has something to do with how Christians are to interpret revelation and apply its message to their day, for it comes at the end of a group of seven parables that do just that for the disciples.
>
> Furthermore, the parable in its context suggests that Jesus is, in some manner, the paradigm for Christian teachers. Just as

Jesus' pattern of ministry is the paradigm for Christian disciple-
ship ('It is enough for the student to be like his teacher, and the
servant like his master' [Matt 10:25]), so Jesus' manner of interpretation is to have some bearing on how Christians interpret
and apply Scripture.[200]

Longenecker does not stand alone here. Keener says, "Jesus expects his
disciples to build on both the biblical teachings that had come before him
and on his gospel of the kingdom."[201] Providing a summary statement of
sorts, Longenecker says that we should understand Matthew 13:52 as Jesus
"giving his immediate disciples—and those who follow them as teachers in
the Christian church—the mandate for a synergistic-developmental model
of contextualizing the early Christian confessions: to bring out of their
storerooms new treasures as well as old!"[202]

Interestingly, Longenecker also mentions John 14:12, which records
Jesus as saying, "Truly, truly, I say to you, he who believes in Me, the works
that I do, he will do also; and greater works than these he will do; because I
go to the Father." Today, we often have a tendency to think in terms of tech-
nological advancements which further the gospel message (e.g., travel abili-
ties, social media, etc.). But Longenecker says, "Jesus' words in John 14:12
should be taken as having principally in mind the recontextualization of the
Christian gospel, a recontextualization that would come about in different
cultures and at later times."[203]

Fifth, *we must remember what Jesus said concerning the arrival of the
Holy Spirit*. While the New Testament presents the truth of a glorious Savior
who reaches out to mankind, it does not always speak directly into modern
situations that were beyond the imagination of the writers. God does not
wish to leave us in the dark and watch us stumble over ourselves. He has left
both his Word and his Spirit, and found within the combination of Word
and Spirit is a light to navigate our way.

As important as the Holy Spirit is to helping us understand Scripture,
many fail to intentionally incorporate the Holy Spirit's guidance into their
interpretive process. This may be the result of insufficient teaching/training,
or it may stem from fear of anything that leans towards the "supernatural."
It can be rooted in church traditions that always stress the Word of God,
while neglecting to acknowledge the arrival of the Holy Spirit that Jesus
emphasized (John 14:16–27; 16:5–15; Acts 1–2). By this, I mean, there is no
real response of the Holy Spirit making a difference in the life of the believer.

We must remember that the sheep know his voice (John 10:3–5, 16,
27), something that is surely possible because of the arrival of the Holy
Spirit. While our confidence in "hearing" the voice of God can sometimes

seem as daunting as application, we must believe Jesus when he said we will know his voice. I will add, however, that "hearing" *must* be coupled with "reading" the Word of God. Hearing that is void of reading often results in many mishandlings of truth.

Finally, the fear sometimes associated with "listening to the Holy Spirit" can also be a reaction against abuses seen in more charismatic circles. Some simply wish to remain as far away from these abuses as possible, not wanting any type of identification with them.

Whatever its root, a fear of or failure to acknowledge the presence of the Holy Spirit in the life of the believer stifles the Spirit's ability to speak new life into the text. The person who does not live as if the Holy Spirit is within them, naturally will hesitate to see application in the text that is not right before their eyes in black and white.

It's imperative that we embrace the presence of the Holy Spirit. Both John 14 and 16 reveal many benefits in doing so. The benefits of Jesus sending the Spirit include:

- The Holy Spirit is a helper (John 14:16, 26; 16:7).

- The Holy Spirit is a Spirit of truth (John 14:17; guides in truth—16:13).

- The Holy Spirit abides in Christians (John 14:17, 20).

- The Holy Spirit is present for us, not leaving us as orphans (John 14:18). This image is more important than we may realize. Jesus did not say, "I'll leave you the New Testament, so just read that and everything will be fine." Instead, Jesus said, "I won't leave you like an orphan who is alone with no parent to guide them. I will send my Spirit."

- The Holy Spirit teaches us (John 14:26).

- The Holy Spirit helps us remember the Word of God (John 14:26).

- The Holy Spirit convicts concerning sin, righteousness, and judgment (John 16:8–11).

- The Holy Spirit makes things known to us (John 16:13–15).

If we wish to make good application of the text, we would be foolish not to consult the Spirit who wants to help guide us in truth. In this, we must wholeheartedly agree with Marshall in that a combination of the Word and "Spirit-given insight"[204] is crucial to making sound application.

2. Metaphor is a means to sound application.

I recently heard Leonard Sweet say, "Metaphors manufacture, manage, and manipulate the world."[205] As an example, he recounted two of President John F. Kennedy's speeches. The first was his famous "moonshot" speech given before Congress on May 25, 1961. Kennedy challenged the nation to land a man on the moon before the decade ended.

The second speech occurred in San Antonio, Texas, on November 21, 1963, the day before Kennedy was assassinated. This brief speech, at the dedication of the Aerospace Medical Health Center, concluded with the following words:

> Many weeks and months and years of long, tedious work lie ahead. There will be setbacks and frustrations and disappointments. There will be, as there always are, pressures in this country to do less in this area as in so many others, and temptations to do something else that is perhaps easier. But this research here must go on. This space effort must go on. The conquest of space must and will go ahead. That much we know. That much we can say with confidence and conviction.
>
> Frank O'Connor, the Irish writer, tells in one of his books how, as a boy, he and his friends would make their way across the countryside, and when they came to an orchard wall that seemed too high and too doubtful to try and too difficult to permit their voyage to continue, they took off their hats and tossed them over the wall—and then they had no choice but to follow them.
>
> This Nation has tossed its cap over the wall of space, and we have no choice but to follow it. Whatever the difficulties, they will be overcome. Whatever the hazards, they must be guarded against. With the vital help of this Aerospace Medical Center, with the help of all those who labor in the space endeavor, with the help and support of all Americans, we will climb this wall with safety and with speed, and we shall then explore the wonders on the other side.[206]

The metaphor of how the nation had "tossed its cap over the wall of space" drove NASA's program for years. And, when Apollo 11 landed the first human on the moon on July 20, 1969, the first words spoken by Neil Armstrong were also metaphor. He said, "That's one small step for man, one giant leap for mankind." Yes, metaphors manufacture, manage, and manipulate the world.

Exploration of biblical metaphors often leads to application. Recognition and use of metaphor can sometimes free the interpreter from the need to "principlize" altogether. Furthermore, use of metaphor employs an existing feature present in the text, thus, one does not have to be concerned with subjectivity issues. In exploring metaphor, the Spirit can help the reader make canonical connections.

Take, for example, Colossians 1:6. Paul says the gospel is "bearing fruit" in the world. The metaphor is so important to Paul, that he repeats it in 1:10 telling the Colossians he prays that they will "bear fruit" in every good work. With a potential thesis to Colossians 1:3–8 being "embrace the gospel and bear fruit," preachers should consider using the metaphor itself to drive home the message. And those studying or reading the passage on their own would do well to give the metaphor more contemplation.

"Fruit" is used metaphorically dozens of times in the New Testament alone. While Galatians 5:22 (the fruit of the Spirit) probably comes to mind quickly, there are many other passages which help one form a good understanding of how the metaphor can be understood. One such example is found in Matthew 3:8. The Pharisees and Sadducees were coming to be baptized by John the Baptist, but when John saw them he called them a "brood of vipers" and told them to "bear fruit in keeping with repentance." In other words, godly fruit begins by turning one's life away from sinful action and towards God. The metaphor is a great application point.

Setting aside, for the moment, the many application theories that have been proposed (i.e., dismissing a method of application that may be viewed by some as problematic), we can safely turn to metaphoric application. As stated in chapter 2, metaphor helps us see beyond the text with imagery that sticks in long-term memory. If we want listeners to apply the text, we should point them towards an image that resonates and can be remembered.

While attending Lincoln Christian Seminary in the late 1990s, I became familiar with the legend of the retired professor James D. Strauss. Having been described by some as the "Einstein of the Restoration Movement," it was not surprising to hear that he was still setting up office in the library. While I never had a Strauss course, a book[207] dedicated to him sparked my interest.

It was the mere title of the book that drew me in: *Taking Every Thought Captive*. The title is grounded in 2 Corinthians 10:5 which says, "We are destroying speculations and every lofty thing raised up against the knowledge of God, and we are taking every thought captive to the obedience of Christ."

The title of the book caused me to stop and consider a text that I must confess, I hadn't previously given a great deal of thought (a little pun, I guess). But I simply could not miss the metaphor plastered right on the front of the book jacket. Paul said we are to take our thoughts "captive." What a powerful and thought-provoking image.

Three metaphorical usages in the New Testament really stand out.

- Luke 4:18—Jesus is reading from Isaiah and says, "He has sent Me to proclaim release to the *captives*, and recovery of sight to the blind, to set free those who are oppressed."

- Colossians 2:8—Paul says, "See to it that no one takes you *captive* through philosophy and empty deception, according to the tradition of men, according to the elementary principles of the world, rather than according to Christ."

- 2 Timothy 2:26—In giving instructions to Timothy, it's of interest to back up to at least verse 23, as it says, "But refuse foolish and ignorant speculations, knowing that they produce quarrels." Paul continues his advice and targets Christian behavior as aiding non-believers in turning to Christ. He says, "perhaps God may grant them repentance leading to the knowledge of the truth, and they come to their senses and escape from the snare of the devil, having been held *captive* by him to do his will."

Before discussing these passages as metaphorical examples, it must be noted that there is a duality to them. In the spiritual realm, all three of these references are literal and not metaphorical. As Paul says in Romans 6:20, before coming to Christ we were all slaves of sin. We were literally bound to sin. Furthermore, we may recount Jesus' words about the truth setting us free, free from sin (John 8:31–36).

But when we take the words at face value, we read them metaphorically, stopping to ask, "What does that word *captive* really represent?" After all, those in attendance at the synagogue (Luke 4) were not physically being held captive. Furthermore, afterwards, Jesus didn't run over to a prison and release a bunch of prisoners. Paul wasn't warning the Colossians about being taken as literal prisoners, and he wasn't telling Timothy that non-believers are being held in a cell by Satan. They, of course, are walking around freely on the streets.

What stands out to me is that the metaphor is so strong, so stimulating, that it's actually easy to forget that it is even metaphor. "Captive" is used to represent those in sin (Luke 4), those being influenced by Satan (2 Tim), those taken by false teaching (Col), and thoughts that drive us from the truth of the gospel (2 Cor).

If we look closely, with exception to Luke 4, all address false teaching that can invade our being. In 2 Corinthians, we read about "speculations" and such that oppose the knowledge of God. In Colossians we read about "philosophies" that deceive. And in 2 Timothy, we again read about "foolish and ignorant speculations" that lead to quarrels, that can cause division. And such division may play right into the hands of the enemy who would love to use others to do his will.

Captivity conjures up different images for different people, and that's okay. While we need to describe aspects of captivity, as a teacher/preacher, it's really unnecessary to define what that exactly looks like. In fact, describing the metaphor in your terms may stifle the imagination of the listener. For example, if you describe captivity as a prison compound, the listener may picture the barbed wire but think to themselves, "Well prisoners get to go outside for recreation, so it may not be that bad." Whereas, left to their own imagination, they may have pictured someone in a cell, or even in solitary confinement.

Resisting the urge to overly describe the metaphor will help the listener make application in terms that mean something to them. Thus, the metaphor serves its purpose by helping the listener picture the dreadful state of captivity.

By concentrating on the metaphor found in 2 Corinthians 10:5, the listener will come to a personal understanding that we must under no circumstances, allow thoughts that oppose God to influence us. Instead of giving the enemy the keys to our mind, we must remember that we (through the power of the Holy Spirit) now hold the keys. We now hold the enemy at bay and lock away false teaching in a cell somewhere, so as to not invade our personal lives.

Notice that I brought the "keys" into the discussion. This is critical as a captive is always looking for the "keys," so to speak. Ultimately, a message of captivity from the Colossians or 2 Timothy texts could turn towards the point in Luke 4, Christ is the key that sets captives free. In 2 Corinthians, however, the point is reversed as we have the ability to hold sinful thoughts or false influences in captivity, away from the life of the Christian. Thus, we are free to live a life that glorifies our lord.

It bears repeating—when present, metaphor is the most powerful application in the text. Let the metaphor, the text, speak for itself. Help your audience understand it but resist overly describing it. Help your audience make the connection and move out of the way and let the Holy Spirit take it from there.

3. On the journey towards application, avoid the detours.

While we may have a lot of questions surrounding how to make application, we can probably all agree that some mistakes simply need to be avoided. Here are a few detours we want to avoid when leading others on the journey of application.

Detour #1—Telling others specifically how to apply the text.

There's a major difference between illustrating how a text may be applied and telling someone exactly how to apply it. Also, when we tell a group of people how they must apply a text, there are bound to be some in the group who cannot relate or simply disagree. Furthermore, if listeners routinely hear restrictive application of the text that does not resonate, they eventually begin losing trust in the preacher/teacher giving such advice.

We should expect people to disagree with hard fast rules of application. After all, people live different lives, with varied challenges and issues. God, in his sovereign wisdom, knows how to help each one of us both uniquely and perfectly. Recognizing individual responsibility before the lord should help one avoid taking this detour and the dead end it leads to for many listeners.

Overdorf offers additional advice when he says,

> Effective sermon application offers possibilities that enhance the work of the Spirit instead of lists that can interfere with the work of the Spirit. We preachers enjoy our lists and steps: "Four things that will give you a vibrant prayer life," or "Three steps to becoming the husband God wants you to be." Such application can limit what the Spirit may want to do with a text in the heart of the listener. What if the Spirit had wanted the listener to implement a fifth 'thing' into her prayer life? What if a husband needed to do something to improve his marriage that the preacher hadn't thought of?[208]

Overdorf's statement about suppressing the Spirit also reminds me of what I said about metaphor. We must resist overly describing everything because it also stifles a person's imagination. When speaking on good writing technique, Stephen King says something similar,

> I can't remember many cases where I felt I had to describe what the people in the story of mine looked like—I'd rather let the reader supply the faces, the builds, and the clothing as well. If I tell you that Carrie White is a high school outcast with a bad

complexion and fashion-victim wardrobe, I think you can do the rest, can't you? I don't need to give you a pimple-by-pimple, skirt-by-skirt rundown. We all remember one or more high school losers, after all; if I describe mine, it freezes out yours.[209]

Giving detailed instruction can be restrictive, even legalistic. Instead, we must give the learner enough information that they themselves can connect the dots. Help send them down a trajectory of thought and allow the Holy Spirit to speak into their lives. We want learners to personalize the message.

Detour #2—Confusing your personal convictions with sound application.

Having observed this mistake over and over, this is a staple item I bring up with all of my students. Note, a person who does this will also insist on taking detour #1. But it is listed independently, because one can travel this detour without taking the first.

We should all have personal convictions and obey what the Holy Spirit is speaking into our lives. Having said that, our convictions are not always the same, because as previously stated, God is working on each one of us in various ways. Let me illustrate.

When I gave my life over to Jesus, I was nineteen years old. Up to that point, a lot of sex-filled, party with the devil, rock and roll invaded my thoughts (e.g., AC/DC's "I'm on the highway to hell"). I felt very strongly that the lord was telling me to get rid of all of my music—yes, all of it.

I went through all my music and separated everything into two piles. In one pile was really bad stuff that I believed nobody should ever listen to. I took those, busted them into pieces, and threw them in a dumpster. I took the other pile and sold it. When I was done, I was literally left with no music.

You can't imagine how much I love music. I estimate that I probably listen to music about 350 days a year (no joke). My wife has even noted that she can shake me out of a foul mood by turning on music. So, discarding an entire music collection was brutal, but I had to obey what I felt the Holy Spirit was telling me.

To fill the void, I turned to contemporary Christian rock. For approximately twenty years, I didn't buy or listen to anything that didn't fall within this genre. I praise the lord for groups like DeGarmo & Key, White Heart and Petra. Their lyrics still speak into my life today.

Now, let's return to "taking every thought captive." My actions could be considered application of this text. And with the strong convictions I held,

I may have been tempted to tell others that they should throw all of their non-Christian music in the dumpster. But while that may not be a bad idea for some, it would be poor instruction on my part.

If I had demanded that everyone live as I do, I would have lost trust with most of my listeners. But for sake of argument, let's say that they all adhered to my application. Wouldn't I also be expected to follow all of their applications as well?

What the lord asked of me was necessary for my growth. However, it is not necessary for everyone. I tend to think the lord has a priority list of growth for each one of us, and as we grow, the lists evolve. What I'm working on today, another may be working on in ten years. In fact, what I'm working on may never be on the list of another, as we all have different vices.

Today, I spend my time listening to about 50 percent secular music and 50 percent Christian. This doesn't mean I'm a hypocrite or a disobedient servant. It simply means that I've learned how to filter out inappropriate music. Just as life is complex and isn't lived out in a black and white world, neither should application be dispensed this way.[210] That type of legalistic living is a detour that leads a person away from Spirit-led living.

Detour #3—Winging it and using the Holy Spirit as an excuse for not preparing.

Uncertainty in application should not be used as an excuse for not contemplating the issues which may be at hand in the text. While the Holy Spirit can most definitely speak "on the spot," teachers should not show up unprepared. I can only assume that such lack of preparation is on account of either ignorance (meaning here, uncertainty in application) or laziness. While the latter is clearly inexcusable, the former is also unfitting to the Christian.

Granted, as a person who has served in local preaching ministry, I know firsthand that preaching weekly presents challenges. Sometimes the problem goes like this—"I spent ten hours preparing this sermon and now I've got to run to the hospital . . . I've got to spend some time with my kids . . . and on and on. What I have done will have to be enough. God will help me with the application while I'm delivering the message."

This is understandable and God knows when we've done our best. But we must remember that winging it can be very dangerous. It's surely one of the reasons Robinson said, "More heresy is preached in application than in Bible exegesis."[211]

When we feel lost in application, it is still wise to listen to Westphal's advice. He says that application is a "matter of good listening, and that is more of a matter of various virtues (openness, honesty, humility, fairness, etc.) than of method. The Word will have to be illuminated by the Spirit, whom Jesus sent to be our teacher; and the Spirit is not a method."[212]

Westphal's words are a reminder that things like attitude and prayer are as important as anything we do. While the Spirit may show up and empower the speaker to "wing it" occasionally, the regular practice of prayer should supersede the regular practice of "winging it." After all, winging it often leads to much harm.

4. Study of the entire canon is imperative—it's the common denominator.

While many have debated how to go about making application, there is a common denominator that has surfaced in the comments of many of the esteemed scholars discussed in this chapter—canonical study. Furthermore, let's not forget that Jesus also used a canonical approach to application (Matt 4:5–7; 12:1–8). This alone is a powerful example that must be considered. Jesus' desire to always see the forest is a lesson well-learned, a lesson that seems to resonate with many. Just a few examples will suffice:

- Webb—He said that his redemptive-movement hermeneutic "investigates the big picture or meta-framework through which we look at Scripture."

- Vanhoozer –He suggested a christological trajectory that employs canonical practice. Furthermore, when speaking of the "drama-of-redemption" model, he said, "We move beyond the script and become faithful performers of the world it implies by cultivating minds nurtured on the canon."

If the book of Hebrews teaches us anything, it's that we can't completely understand the New Testament without first comprehending the Old Testament. Moreover, Jesus made it clear that he didn't come to abolish the Law or the Prophets, but to fulfill them (Matt 5:17). Sound application never takes place among the trees, it must be discovered in the forest.

5. The Holy Spirit has arrived, making canonical study alone insufficient.

Studying the entirety of Scripture naturally leads a person to consider trajectory of thought. After all, as one studies the development from Old to New, the concept of advancement begins to invade a person's thinking. Within this context, it only seems natural to inquire as to what the arrival of the Holy Spirit also means.

The Christian life is one of Spirit activity. While it must be admitted that complete controls to application can only take place through and "within" complete canonical study, Christians are not to live a rigid "Bible-only" life. The Christian life consists of both Bible and Spirit.

While the New Testament is the primary guide to understanding the will of God for our lives, we must interact with the words and see that the text is meant to live and breathe. Jesus sent his Holy Spirit for a reason. Christians are to hear and obey the voice of the Shepherd, and the hearing goes beyond the literal words we read on paper.

As discussed earlier, this leaning into the area of the working of the Holy Spirit can be uncomfortable, and at times, even frightening. Additionally, it means that establishing complete controls over application becomes impossible. To that I would just say, "Welcome to the Christian life." We all wish God would write a single, personalized volume for each one of us, one that would simply tell us what to do all the time. But he hasn't chosen to do that.

Yes, I realize here that some will say, "He did, he gave us the Bible." Such a statement is simply not true. The Bible doesn't tell me if I should quit my job and move to another. The Bible doesn't tell me which person I should marry. And the Bible doesn't tell me how many children I should have. The issues just go on and on. But this is precisely why God sent his Spirit to us.

Some readers might respond by thinking to themselves, "Application of the text is not always the same as application to life situations." This is obviously true[213] and perhaps I've crossed over from interpretive application to living the Christian life. But in all honesty, how does a Christian cleanly separate the two? We read the Bible so that we know how to live. Indeed, the question of application is a messy one.

Still, the Spirit not only affirms and helps us recall the truths we read in God's Word, but also speaks into our lives in a personal way. God is not off in some corner of the universe hiding from us. He lives within us and wants to commune with us in a personal way. This, of course, takes application to very uncomfortable places, and part of the discomfort involves the trajectory of biblical principles.

Trajectory is an important concept. Casillas mentions the late Supreme Court Judge Antonin Scalia, and how trajectory impacts constitutional interpretation. The mere mention of this may alienate some who will automatically associate such practice as liberalism at its worst. Scalia, however, was a conservative nominated by Ronald Reagan. In fact, Scalia was a "textualist," meaning he believed interpretation and application of the law should be grounded in the Constitution itself. Yet he said the following,

> Sometimes (though not very often) there will be disagreement regarding the original meaning and sometimes there will be disagreement as to how the original meaning applies to new and unforeseen circumstances. . . . [in some situations] the Court must follow the trajectory of the First Amendment, so to speak, to determine what it requires—and assuredly that enterprise is not entirely cut-and-dried but requires the exercise of judgment.[214]

Like conservative Christians who want to align their lives with the biblical witness, Scalia wanted to apply law that was also based on the written text. Yet, in his conservativism, he essentially encountered the same problems we do. The text, even when written with the future in mind, is time bound to the culture of its day, making clear black and white interpretation to be a daunting task. Scalia knew that at times you need to see beyond the text.

I find both France's idea of "trajectory" and Webb's concept of "seed ideas" insightful. While they both lack the "controls" we seek, we must again remind ourselves that the Holy Spirit is our Helper who wants to assist us in understanding the spirit of the text.

We should ask questions like, "Is Galatians 3:28 just good theology? Should I respond to it? And if so, how?" When we are dismissive of the text as something that only informs but does not drive us to action, we have a problem. Such a problem could be equated to knowing we should forgive someone but refusing to do so. Canonical study combined with Spirit-infused activity should be our goal, a goal that results in action/application.

6. We must tell God's story with relevance, as relevance leads to application.

Preacher Floyd Bresee, said it this way, "When you preach, don't aim to lecture on the water of life, but to give your listeners a drink."[215]

Halford E. Luccock illustrates[216] by postulating a scenario in which someone is speaking to a man dying of thirst in the Sahara: "Let us consider the properties of what we call water. Water is a colorless liquid which on being raised to a temperature of 212 degrees Fahrenheit . . . becomes what is called vapour. If, however, on the other hand, the temperature is lowered to 32 degrees Fahrenheit, lo, it is ice. In the final analysis it is discovered to consist of two portions of hydrogen to one of oxygen, hence arises the name H_2O."

A thirsty man interrupts, "For the love of God, mister, give me a drink!"

We might say that what lacks in a great deal of sermons is that we never get around to helping people take a drink. Sermons should not only educate the mind but jolt the heart and move people to action. And to do that, listeners must first see that the message maintains some relevance. Here are some issues to consider:

- A message that is difficult to follow and has no clear point will naturally not be considered relevant or applied. By contrast, the chances of being relevant are boosted if a message is clear and actually going somewhere.

- Does the message relate to real life? Does it somehow speak into the lives of the listeners?

- Does the message challenge me, encourage me, inspire me, correct me, stir me? Does it create behavioral modification? Cause me to hunger?

- Does the message speak to the tensions in life?

Relevance leads to application, and that should never be forgotten. This is where narrative and metaphor come back into play. People relate to both stories and images, as they stir the imagination. For example's sake, let's consider Genesis 37, the story of Joseph and his robe of many colors.

While this is narrative, we often shortchange the story by turning it into three propositional points. Narrative isn't to be turned into a few nice points that people will forget in 10 minutes anyway. Narrative speaks to the tensions in life, tensions that we can often relate to. In this particular story, the tension is off the charts.

- Joseph brings a bad report about his brothers to his father, Jacob (he breaks the "keep this between us" code).

- Jacob loves Joseph more than his brothers (favoritism problems).

- Joseph walks around with his super cool robe (favoritism problems, potential arrogance issues, lack of wisdom).

- Joseph's brothers hate him.

- Joseph has a dream where everyone serves him . . . now his brothers hate him even more *(lack of wisdom and lack of control over his tongue)*.

- When we finally get to verse 11 (yes, all of this tension in just 11 verses) we read that his brothers are jealous of him.

- By the time we get to verse 18, Joseph's brothers are plotting to kill him.

We've got trust issues, favoritism, arrogance, hatred, communication problems, jealousy, and even murderous thoughts. Now this is what I call tension, and it's the tensions in life that everyone can relate to. When you tell a story like this, there's not a person in the audience who isn't engaged, well, unless you rigidly stare at your Bible the entire time and read it like you do the newspaper.

Reuben, the oldest brother, comes to the rescue. Instead of killing Joseph, Reuben convinces them to sell him into slavery. Now here's my point. A great many preachers would turn this into a three-point sermon on something like the "Providence of God" or "The Penalties Associated with Bad Parenting."

But if we're to be true to the literary form, we should focus on the conflict, the tension. Think of this story through Joseph's eyes. "I was just living my life to the best of my ability. I can't help it that my Dad loves me. I didn't deserve to be sold into slavery. I miss my family. Where is God in the midst of this madness I've walked into?"

We might say, "A lot of life doesn't seem to make sense. You make plans, but they don't come about. You're true to God, but you aren't rewarded for it. If that's where you are, here's a man in Joseph who experienced that . . . here's a man you can relate to."[217]

The conflict Joseph encountered is real life and, therefore, relevant. As preachers, we need to help people make that connection. Karl Barth once described preaching as an attempt to give God's answers to the questions people raise. Going back to Joseph, as a preacher I would want to try to help people answer these difficult questions like, "Where was God when . . . ?"

Preaching with relevance is hard work. We need to recognize that and learn to be comfortable with not always giving the perfect application of the text. Remember, what we may think is perfect application may be completely irrelevant to someone else.

We need to give explanation of the text followed with implications that will then send the listener off into a personal trajectory of relevance, causing them to make personal application.

Let's be honest. Some people don't mind being told what to do. After all, it's easier than thinking for yourself. But it's not our job to merely indoctrinate people and turn them into clones that follow our strict behavioral guidelines. We need to get people to interact with both the Word of God and the Holy Spirit. We need to get people to seek God in prayer so that he can guide their lives with the personal touch they desperately need.

7. We should run all application through the filter of Matthew 22:36–40.

In Matthew 22:36–40, Jesus was asked about the greatest commandment in the Law. His response was, "You shall love the lord your God with all your heart, and with all your soul, and with all your mind." Then he said the second is like it, "You shall love your neighbor as yourself."

Jesus went on to say that the Law and Prophets hang on these commandments, so just imagine how imperative these two commandments are! Loving God and loving others is what it's all about.[218] Sometimes we overly complicate matters. These two items should always be at the forefront of our thinking.

Running all of our potential applications through this filter is essential. After all, it's a good idea to cover the essentials; we might be surprised how often these actually make a big difference.

FINAL THOUGHTS

It's worth repeating—God has not called us to hoard knowledge, he has called us to application of that knowledge. But the difficulty with knowing how to responsibly apply Scripture is evident by the lack of books on the topic. Thus, searching for a clear process is as elusive as the fountain of youth. We must concede that application often lies in the world of "art," a place most biblical scholars are not really comfortable.

Surely, God understands our angst. He understands our desire to adhere to and obey his truth. In response, his Spirit goes with us. We must not fear the absence of certainty. Jesus is the way, the truth, and the life. We only need to follow closely and he will help us see into the depths.

Conclusion

AFTER I WROTE THE first draft of this book, I kept attempting to see a Magic Eye image. One night, as my wife and I were sitting together in the living room, she gave me her phone and asked me try a few of the images she had just observed. By holding the image as close to my nose as possible, trying to look through the image, and slowly pulling it away from myself, I was able to see a few images. But after about five seconds, as my eyes refocused, I kept losing the image. A few months later that technique no longer worked for me.

So, I got back online and found the "crossed eyes" method.[219] Starting with what a website called "easier ones," I had success! Of course, crossing your eyes isn't the most comfortable exercise, but at least it worked. With this method I was able to see a 3D image that had four layers of depth. In fact, once I saw the image I could not unsee it until I completely turned my eyes away.

I find my experience as an illustration for Bible readers. There is a depth of riches that, if seen, helps us interact with the text with new excitement. Once we see the depths of the text, we enter new venues for discussion that move us past word-only contemplation, black and white reading, tree living, and static application.

If we are to engage a culture that is becoming more and more disinterested in Christianity, we must speak a language that engages them. At this point, it's pretty clear that non-believers are not interested in church events that feature word driven three-point sermons that fail to grip the imagination of the listener, that fail to move past cultural boundaries, and that fail to portray the liberating good news of the gospel. These messages are as quickly forgotten as the headline in yesterday's newspaper.

Furthermore, they aren't exactly captivated by a Christianity which features a Bible that appears "out of touch." As some hang on to supposed "literal" readings that fail to speak into present day life, they are hindering non-believers from experiencing the fullness and life of the sacred text. Our

God must be presented as one who "gets it," and often our problem is that we simply don't.

Consider that God gave us a Bible rich in imagery and narrative. Consider that God works within culture but is not stuck within any particular place or time. Consider that Jesus is the truth, and tree dwelling is unfit for the lord of the Cosmos. Consider that the Holy Spirit has never been static and does not intend on changing anytime soon.

We must think bigger than words, cultures, single texts, and static applications. After all, our God is a big God who is always bent on moving us forward. Big thinking is exactly where God dwells. And in God's big plan, he still works to reach unbelievers who are turned off to both the church and the Bible. Since God chooses to use his people to share the good news, we must share it with a newfound vision, a vision that brings the depths into focus.

Endnotes

CHAPTER 1

1. Wikipedia, "Johannes Gutenberg," paragraph 2.
2. Guinness World Records, "Best Selling Book," paragraph 1.
3. Unless otherwise noted, all biblical quotes are taken from the New American Standard Bible. Most of the time, I have removed the italics and CAPS they sometimes incorporate into the text.
4. I completed my Doctor of Ministry at Portland Seminary of George Fox University under Dr. Sweet and have heard him provide many great examples.
5. Revelation 12:3
6. My wife Lisa says, "I'm thinking of the cushion being a sign of intention too. It's not like Jesus is so tired he just crashed. No, he grabbed a cushion and got all settled in."

CHAPTER 2

7. Expository sermons are the result of careful exegesis (exegesis is "drawing out" the meaning) of a passage of study. In the expository sermon, the text is exposed to the listener.
8. Wilmes, et al., "Coming to Our Senses," 659–66.
9. Parsons, "Do Visuals Really Trump Text?," paragraph 15.
10. Grady, et al., "Neural Correlates of the Episodic Encoding of Pictures and Words," 2703–08.
11. Clarkson, "12 Hard Stats that Proof the Power of Images," point 9.
12. Sweet estimates that as much as 75 percent of the Bible is made up of narrative, story which appeals to the imagination. Sweet, VLOG episode 7.
13. Julicher set forth that parables have just one meaning (one large extended simile). While others such as C. H. Dodd and Joachim Jeremias built on Julicher's effort, Craig Blomberg's work (*Interpreting the Parables*, 1990) greatly influences interpreters today. Blomberg believes there are simple parables with one single point (e.g., Matt 13:44–46), parables with two points (e.g., Matt 24:43–44; Luke 12:39–40), and yet more complex parables with three points (e.g., Matt 20:1–16). Blomberg's method reveals the parable of the Prodigal Son as a triadic (three points) parable with the rebellious son, the forgiving father, and the resentful brother each teaching a significant point. It's the complex nature of some parables that explains why preachers often disagree as to what

the big point is; sometimes there is simply more than one.

14. Geary, *I Is an Other*, 10.

15. Lakoff and Johnson, *Metaphors We Live By,* 2nd ed., 6.

16. While I've read this example before (but don't remember where), I will say that I remember Leonard Sweet discussing this one day in class.

17. Kaiser Jr., et al, eds, *NIV Archaeological Study Bible*, 2,015.

CHAPTER 3

18. Kuhatschek, *Applying the Bible*, 37–38.

19. God Bringing Israel Out of Egypt, "Knowing Jesus."

20. Womble, *Beyond Reasonable Doubt*, 176.

21. Womble, *Beyond Reasonable Doubt*, 178.

22. France, *Women in the Church's Ministry*, 57–58.

23. Womble, *Beyond Reasonable Doubt*, 178.

24. Keener, "An Egalitarian View," 29.

25. Womble, *Beyond Reasonable Doubt*, 175–209.

26. Craig Keener is just one of many commentators to point this out. Keener, *A Commentary on the Gospel of Matthew*, 477.

27. Kaiser Jr., *Hard Sayings of the Bible*, 175–76.

28. Womble, *Beyond Reasonable Doubt*, 315.

29. For a more complete discussion, see Womble, *Beyond Reasonable Doubt*, 309–17.

30. Womble, *Beyond Reasonable Doubt*, 315.

31. Lowery, *Revelation's Rhapsody*, 55.

32. Lowery, *Revelation's Rhapsody*, 55.

33. Renowned scholar F. F. Bruce once published a book, *The Hard Sayings of Jesus* (1983). Bruce had said that "they may be hard for two different reasons. First are those that, because of differences in culture and time, are hard to understand without having their social and historical backgrounds explained. Second are those that are all too easily understood but that challenge the ways we think and act." Eventually five total books were written by various authors. Today, there is a single volume called, *Hard Sayings of the Bible*. Kaiser Jr. et al., *Hard Sayings of the Bible*.

34. Richards & O' Brien, *Misreading Scripture with Western Eyes*, 113.

35. I believe I first saw this explanation in the following: Wilson, *Our Father Abraham*. I have since seen it in other sources too.

36. Dearman, "Sodom," 974.

37. DeadSea.com, "Why is the Dead Sea Called the Dead Sea?," paragraph 12.

38. Kidner, *Genesis*, 146.

CHAPTER 4

39. I do not recall where I saw this.

40. For several years now, I've been using the following with my students. It's very user-friendly and doesn't speak over the reader. Duvall and Hays, *Grasping God's Word*.

41. Bible readers are often encouraged to read three chapters each day to get through the entire Bible in one-year. While this is a great plan for new readers, such a plan must be abandoned for serious readers. Take the book of Acts as an example. Under the previously mentioned plan, it would take nine days to read Acts. But the reality is that

you can read Acts in two hours or less. You'll see things by the reading the book in one sitting that you would never see over a nine-day period. Most importantly, you'll see the overarching themes much more clearly.

42. Burge, *The New Testament in Seven Sentences*, 63–66.

43. A simple chiasm can be seen in following quote by President Kennedy:

A Ask not what your *country*

    B can do for *you*

    B but what *you* can do

A for your *country*

44. Womble, *Beyond Reasonable Doubt*, 190.

45. Womble, *Beyond Reasonable Doubt*, 198.

46. Womble, *Beyond Reasonable Doubt*, 208.

47. Womble, *Beyond Reasonable Doubt*, 291–93.

48. Womble, *Beyond Reasonable Doubt*, 180.

49. The ESV notes, "The Greek word *anthropoi* can refer to both men and women, depending on the context." This is why, for example, the NIV says "people."

50. It must be acknowledged that there is some uncertainty surrounding if whether Paul actually wrote this letter to the Ephesians. A textual variant is present in 1:1, in that the words "at Ephesus" are not present in some early manuscripts. Nevertheless, Metzger says the committee had difficulty in deciding which reading is correct but decided to retain the words. They did, however, place the words in brackets. Metzger, *A Textual Commentary on the Greek New Testament*.

51. Womble, *Beyond Reasonable Doubt*, 244.

52. Womble, *Beyond Reasonable Doubt*, 246.

53. Womble, *Beyond Reasonable Doubt*. I address these women at length, 285–98.

54. Womble, *Beyond Reasonable Doubt*, 299.

55. Womble, *Beyond Reasonable Doubt*, 300–01.

56. Womble, *Beyond Reasonable Doubt*, 216.

57. Womble, *Beyond Reasonable Doubt*, 212.

58. Womble, *Beyond Reasonable Doubt*, 215.

59. Blomberg, *1 Corinthians*, 214.

60. Womble, *Beyond Reasonable Doubt*, 224.

61. Womble, *Beyond Reasonable Doubt*, 223–42.

62. Womble, *Beyond Reasonable Doubt*, 309–17.

63. Womble, *Beyond Reasonable Doubt*, 319.

64. Grenz with Kjesbo, *Women in the Church*, 78.

65. Witherington III, *Women in the Earliest Churches*, 156.

66. Staton, *The Biblical Liberation of Women for Leadership in the Church*, 120.

67. Womble, *Beyond Reasonable Doubt*, 298.

68. Staton, *The Biblical Liberation of Women for Leadership in the Church*, 48.

69. Womble, *Beyond Reasonable Doubt*, 33.

70. Womble, *Beyond Reasonable Doubt*, 39.

France, *Women in the Church's Ministry*, 92.

71. I believe I found this nice phrase in one of my books, but I'm simply unable to locate it.

CHAPTER 5

72. Stein, *A Basic Guide to Interpreting the Bible*, 75.

73. A possible exception to knowing the rules might take place when reading opinion/editorials. Some people get mad at the newspaper because they consider an editorial the opinion of the paper/organization as a whole, when in fact it is not.

74. Vanhoozer, *Pictures at a Theological Exhibition*, 75.

75. Vanhoozer, *Pictures at a Theological Exhibition*, 75.

76. Both Duvall and Hays, *Grasping God's Word* and Klein, et al., *Introduction to Biblical Interpretation* agree on these nine major categories. They are substantial books in the field of hermeneutics.

77. Revelation 1:1–6 reveals that three primary literary forms are present: letter, prophecy, and revelation (or apocalypse). And because modern readers are completely unfamiliar with apocalyptic literature (symbols, visions, metaphors, images, and other worldly beings), reading with understanding can be frustrating.

78. Phenomenological language describes something from our perspective and does not necessarily convey how things actually are (the reality). For example, Joshua 10:12–13 recounts how Joshua prayed and then the "sun stood still." Critics of the Bible are quick to point out this scientific problem, since the sun always stands still. However, there's nothing unusual in describing things in this manner. Just consider the beautiful "sunset" you may see.

79. Anthropomorphic language describes God in human terms (e.g., his hands, feet, mouth, etc.).

80. The synoptics are Matthew, Mark, and Luke. There are similar accounts of the good news of Christ.

81. The most popular book on this topic is the following: Fee and Stuart, *How to Read the Bible for All Its Worth*. I also like Duvall and Hays, *Grasping God's Word*. They give a full chapter in their textbook to each of the nine primary literary forms, about 230 pages.

82. Craigie, *Psalms 1–50*, 41.

83. Fee and Stuart, *How to Read the Bible for All It's Worth*, 195.

84. Ewert, *How to Understand the Bible*, 146.

85. In a nutshell, Calvinism teaches that God chooses his elect. By contrast, an Arminian position is that each person has a free choice in the matter.

86. Carson, *Exegetical Fallacies*, 137.

87. Carson, *Exegetical Fallacies*, 138.

88. Todd, "Who Was Canadian Behind Iconic Image of 'Laughing Jesus?'"

89. *The Visual Bible: Matthew*, DVD, directed by Regardt van den Bergh.

90. Jesus used a variety of means to capture attention, things such as hyperbole (gross exaggeration), overstatement, understatement (litotes), and puns.

91. Stein, *The Method and Message of Jesus' Teachings*, 11.

92. Curry, "Pujols's Shot Recedes in Lidge's Review Mirror," paragraph 9.

93. There is some debate about verse 22. For example, was the father even dead? Or did Jesus see some poor intentions like he did with the Rich Young Ruler? While I find these discussions interesting, I still conclude that this is Jesus utilizing his love for hyperbole.

94. Keener, *The IVP Bible Background Commentary*, 94.

95. Bruce, *The Hard Sayings of Jesus* (1983) which is now found in the new compilation book, *Hard Sayings of the Bible*, 438.

96. This is a comment she made to me while editing this book.

97. Duvall and Hays, *Grasping God's Word*, 293.

98. Fee and Stuart, *How to Read the Bible for All It's Worth*, 97.

99. Duvall and Hays, *Grasping God's Word*, 300–06.

100. Klein, et al., *Introduction to Biblical Interpretation*, 539–40.

CHAPTER 6

101. Westphal, "The Philosophical/Theological Response," 162.

102. Overdorf, *Applying the Sermon*, 56–57.

103. Veerman, *How to Apply the Bible*, 49.

104. Veerman, *How to Apply the Bible*, 35–53.

105. Veerman, *How to Apply the Bible*, 47.

106. Klein, et al., *Introduction to Biblical Interpretation*, 605.

107. Webb, *Slaves, Women & Homosexuals*, 13.

108. Two examples: McQuilken, *Understanding and Applying the Bible*, 306. Casillas, *Beyond Chapter and Verse*, 254, shows a partial process.

109. Porter, "Hermeneutics, Biblical Interpretation, and Theology: Hunch, Holy Spirit, or Hard Work?," 121.

110. Several have tackled this issue, such as Fee and Stuart (*How to Read the Bible for All Its Worth*), Osborne (*The Hermeneutical Spiral*), Virkler (*Hermeneutics*), and Webb (*Slaves, Women & Homosexuals*). One to certainly consult is Klein, et al., *Introduction to Biblical Interpretation*, 602–36.

111. Muller, *The Study of Theology*, 198.

112. Longenecker says that Adolf Harnack popularized this approach (lectures from 1899 to 1900 found in the book *What is Christianity?*). Longenecker, *New Testament Social Ethics for Today*, 3.

113. Kaiser Jr., *Toward an Exegetical Theology*, 152. See also, Kaiser Jr., "A Principlizing Model," 19–50.

114. Here are a few that also discuss identifying the principles: McQuilken (*Understanding and Applying the Bible*), Veerman (*How to Apply the Bible*), Doriani (*Putting the Truth to Work*). Klein, et al., (*Introduction to Biblical Interpretation*), Virkler (*Hermeneutics*), and Duvall and Hays (*Grasping God's Word*). Robinson's "abstraction ladder" is essentially the same (sounds like the "principlizing bridge" Duvall and Hays present) in that he attempts to ascertain the "text's intent." Robinson, "The Heresy of Application," 20–27. Also, Robinson and Larson, eds., *The Art and Craft of Biblical Preaching*. Kaiser Jr. says (in "A Principlizing Model," 24) that the "Ladder of Abstraction" was first presented by Schuter and Clements, *Toward Rediscovering the Old Testament*, 164–66.

115. Kuhatschek, *Applying the Bible*, 37–86.

116. Kuhatschek, *Applying the Bible*, 57–61.

117. McQuilken, *Understanding and Applying the Bible*, 300–06.

118. Veerman, *How to Apply the Bible*, 49.

119. Duvall and Hays, *Grasping God's Word*, 200–01.

120. Kaiser Jr. explains the "Ladder of Abstraction" in "A Principlizing Model," in *Four Views on Moving Beyond the Bible to Theology*, 19–50. He says to work from the *ancient specific situation* up the ladder to the *institutional or personal norm*, to the top of the ladder which gives the *general principle*. As one descends the ladder, the *theological and moral principle* behind the general principle is discovered. Then one descends further to the contemporary or New Testament *specific situation*.

121. Robinson, *The Heresy of Application*, 20–27.

122. As an example, Virkler provides five guidelines for principlizing. Virkler, *Hermeneutics*, 200.

123. Clark, *To Know and Love God*, 91–98, (as cited in Vanhoozer, "Into the Great Beyond," 92).

124. Doriani believes narrative can also be used to draw principles. He says, "The principle is clear: Where a series of acts by the faithful create a pattern, and God or the narrator approves the pattern, it directs believers, even if no law spells out the lesson."

Doriani, "A Redemptive-Historical Model," 89.

125. Vanhoozer, "Into the Great Beyond," 92.

126. Longenecker, *New Testament Social Ethics for Today*, 16–28.

127. Longenecker, *New Testament Social Ethics for Today*, 14–15. (1) Ethical statements of the New Testament are to be taken with prescriptive and obligatory force, and not just as tactical suggestions. (2) The ethical statements of the New Testament are given not as detailed codes of conduct but as principles or precepts which seek primarily to set a standard for the kind of life pleasing to God, to indicate the direction we ought to be moving, and to signal the quality of life our actions ought to be expressing. (3) For there to be an ethic that in any sense can be called Christian, there must be the direct action of the Holy Spirit in the Christian's life and in the particular circumstances confronted. Indeed, not only does the Spirit regenerate; he also gives guidance as to how the principles of Christ should be applied in given situations and empowers the Christian to put these directives into effect. (4) For any action to be truly Christian, it must be expressive of a relationship with God through Christ and must work itself out with attention to the specific situations it encounters, always motivated and conditioned by love for God and love for one's fellows.

128. It should be noted that Longenecker was not speaking of principlizing (finding the principle from the text). He was speaking of ethical statements as principles.

129. Longenecker, *New Testament Social Ethics for Today*, 25.

130. Longenecker, *New Testament Social Ethics for Today*, 26.

131. During the editing process, my wife Lisa gave me most of this sentence.

132. Longenecker, *New Testament Social Ethics for Today*, 22–23.

133. Longenecker, *New Testament Social Ethics for Today*, 27.

134. "Contextualization" is essentially about taking the biblical message into a new environment and making it relevant. Longenecker, *New Wine into Fresh Wineskins*, 136–53.

135. Longenecker, *New Wine into Fresh Wineskins*, 140. The three weaknesses are: "First, this model often finds it difficult to discern between the essential principles and the situational-cultural wrapping of the biblical message. Second, in its biblical interpretation it often treats Scripture in a rather static fashion, without giving any credence to developments between the testaments or to differences within the testaments. Third, it all-too-often assumes the ability of outside experts to understand and decode the perspectives, customs, and cultures of the recipients, and so it can make rather superficial judgments about the meaning of certain images and the interrelationship of certain ideas of the receptor people."

136. Longenecker, *New Wine into Fresh Wineskins*, 147–48.

137. Longenecker, *New Wine into Fresh Wineskins*, 148.

138. Longenecker, *New Wine into Fresh Wineskins*, 148–49.

139. France, *Women in the Church's Ministry*, 22, 92.

140. France, *Women in the Church's Ministry*, 24.

141. France, *Women in the Church's Ministry*, 24.

142. Webb, *Slaves, Women & Homosexuals*.

143. Webb, *Slaves, Women & Homosexuals*, 16.

144. Webb, *Slaves, Women & Homosexuals*, 30.

145. Webb, *Slaves, Women & Homosexuals*, 30.

146. Webb, *Slaves, Women & Homosexuals*, 30–31.

147. Webb, *Slaves, Women & Homosexuals*, 31.

148. Webb, *Slaves, Women & Homosexuals*, 54.

149. Webb, *Slaves, Women & Homosexuals*, 53.

150. Webb, *Slaves, Women & Homosexuals*, 53.

151. Webb, *Slaves, Women & Homosexuals*, 32.

152. Webb, *Slaves, Women & Homosexuals*, 34.

153. Webb, *Slaves, Women & Homosexuals*, 73.

154. Webb, *Slaves, Women & Homosexuals*, 83.

155. Webb, *Slaves, Women & Homosexuals*, 110.

156. Webb, "A Redemptive-Movement Model," 215–48.

157. Webb, "A Redemptive-Movement Model," 215.

158. Webb, "A Redemptive-Movement Model," 216.

159. Webb, "A Redemptive-Movement Model," 217.

160. Webb, "A Redemptive-Movement Model," 221.

161. Webb, "A Redemptive-Movement Model," 245.

162. Webb, "A Redemptive-Movement Model," 246.

163. Webb, "A Redemptive-Movement Model," 226.

164. Marshall, *Beyond the Bible*, 71.

165. Marshall, *Beyond the Bible*, 73.

166. Marshall, *Beyond the Bible*, 35.

167. Marshall, *Beyond the Bible*, 61. Marshall adds (61–62), "If the proposals in Acts 15 were intended simply to provide a modus vivendi for Gentiles living with law-keeping Jewish Christians (as Acts 15:21 might be taken to suggest), they are not necessary if the situation changes. . . . So the question arises of whether we are to see a theology in process of transition. The fact that many millions of Gentile Christians of many denominations do not confine themselves to kosher meat shows that the church has not regarded the decree as an unchangeable law."

168. Marshall, *Beyond the Bible*, 77.

169. Marshall, *Beyond the Bible*, 78–79. Marshall's seven points he hopes to have established are: (1) There is development in doctrine throughout the Bible leading to diversity and greater maturity in teaching at different states, although the later is not necessarily more mature than the earlier. (2) There is an incompleteness in Scripture, seen in factors such as the diversity, the occasional nature of the teaching, and the impossibility of dealing with later questions and problems, all of which mean that doctrine can and must develop beyond scriptural statements. (3) Since the revelation is given not simply in individual texts as units of meaning, but through the whole of Scripture, the individual texts must be seen in light of the whole, and some may be seen as staging posts on the way to fuller understanding; they are no longer valid in their original form, although they were once authoritative in that form, but continue to be authoritative in a different way. (4) There is continuity throughout the process. The God of the Old Testament is the same God as in the New Testament and acts in essentially the same ways. Likewise, the teaching of Jesus stands in continuity with the Old Testament and the teaching of the early church; and within the developments in the early church there is a firm understanding of the "gospel" as a given. (5) The development is controlled by various principles: the shift from the old covenant to the new covenant; the shift from the liminal period *(he means the teachings of Jesus)* to the early church; the facing of new situations, new currents of thought, new errors, and the like. (6) Developments in doctrine and new understandings after the closing of the canon are inevitable. These must be based on continuity with the faith once given to God's people, and must be in accordance with what I have called "the mind of Christ." They may relativize some aspects of biblical teaching that was appropriate for specific occasions and cultural settings or where the gospel itself (and not some modern or postmodern agenda) requires us to do so. (7) In this way, we affirm the ongoing supreme authority of Scripture, but we recognize that Scripture needs interpretation and fresh application, both in our doctrine and in our practice.

170. Vanhoozer, "Into the Great Beyond," 91–92.

171. Vanhoozer, "Into the Great Beyond," 91.

172. Vanhoozer, "Into the Great Beyond," 93.

173. Vanhoozer, "Into the Great Beyond," 94.

174. Vanhoozer, "Into the Great Beyond," 94.

175. Wright, *The Last Word*.

176. Wright, *The Last Word*, 18–19.

177. Wright, *The Last Word*, 18–19.

178. Wright, *The Last Word*, 122.

179. Wright, *The Last Word*, 121.

180. Wright, *The Last Word*, 126.

181. Wright, *The Last Word*, 126–27.

182. Wright, *The Last Word*, 135.

183. Wright, *The Last Word*, 135.

184. Vanhoozer, "A Drama-of-Redemption Model," 151–99.

185. Vanhoozer, "A Drama-of-Redemption Model," 155.

186. Vanhoozer, "A Drama-of-Redemption Model," 156.

187. Vanhoozer, "A Drama-of-Redemption Model," 167.

188. Vanhoozer, "A Drama-of-Redemption Model," 168.

189. Vanhoozer, "A Drama-of-Redemption Model," 158–59.

190. Vanhoozer, "A Drama-of-Redemption Model," 169–72.

191. Vanhoozer, "A Drama-of-Redemption Model," 170. Vanhoozer quotes: Briggs, *Reading the Bible*, 95.

192. Vanhoozer, "A Drama-of-Redemption Model," 170–71.

193. Vanhoozer, "A Drama-of-Redemption Model," mentions other approaches in "A Drama-of-Redemption Model," 157: history-of-redemption, narrative-of-redemption, and logic-of-redemption. I also exclude Doriani's "redemptive-historical" model, as seen in Doriani, "A Redemptive-Historical Model." Because he spends a great deal of time criticizing others, it is difficult to ascertain the model he offers. He implies that his method begins with taking the text at "face value" (79). When discussing what he describes as Step 3: Application of Scripture, he also says that the "imitation of God/imitation of Christ motif pervades Scripture and is a leading source of ethical guidance" (86). And in Step 4; Adjusting a Traditional View of Application, he notes that narrative is a source for drawing application (86–89). He concludes by saying that his "proposal is essentially a call to return to diligent exegesis and the orthodoxies of interpretation" (118). This statement is telling in that Doriani focuses mostly on exegesis and never fully explains his model for making application.

I would also like to note Porter's *"Pauline model."* He notes that Paul's thought was driven by three beliefs: God (his activity in the world), Christ (we in some way all participate in his death and resurrection), and last of all, that as Christians follow after Christ, Christ will be seen in their lives. Porter says (124) that while Paul's "hermeneutical principles were complex . . . a couple of them are worth noting." First, Paul was "able to differentiate between what was essential and what was contingent in the text. He can cite specific examples from the Old Testament without their specificity holding back the meaning of the text for his contemporary situation." And second, "Paul can pay attention to each letter without becoming overly literalistic."

Porter (125) anticipates the next question and asks, "What about the understanding of the New Testament, where we have no subsequent testament to guide our interpretation?" To this, Porter turns to the translational method of *dynamic equivalence*. He maintains that it is not only a task of translation, but of theology. In summarizing the theory (125–27) behind dynamic equivalence, he says one must determine the "kernel or heart" of what is being said in the original text. While in translation this is limited to a sentence, Porter explains that the theory can be applied to larger units of thought. He maintains that this process will reveal biblical relevance. Porter, "Hermeneutics, Biblical Interpretation, and Theology: Hunch, Holy Spirit, or Hard Work?"

194. Webb also notes this observation. Webb, "A Redemptive-Movement Model," 242.

195. Webb, "A Redemptive-Movement Model," 217.

196. Alvord, "The Question of Application in Preaching,"136.

197. Longenecker, *New Wine into Fresh Wineskins*, 151.

198. Longenecker, *New Wine into Fresh Wineskins*, 132.

199. Marshall, *The Gospel of Luke*, 227–28.

200. Longenecker, *New Wine into Fresh Wineskins*, 151–52.

201. Keener, *A Commentary on the Gospel of Matthew*, 393.

202. Longenecker, *New Wine into Fresh Wineskins*, 175.

203. Longenecker, *New Wine into Fresh Wineskins*, 175.

204. I greatly appreciate Longenecker's (*New Testament Social Ethics for Today*, 13) insights. He says, "Paul puts to the fore in discussing the issues at Corinth and that which distinguishes Christian ethics from all forms of legalism and Stoicism: immediate and personal direction by God through His Holy Spirit (cf. 1 Cor. 2:10–16). Paul identifies this feature of Christian living as the 'mind of Christ" (*nous Christou*), meaning by that Christ's example and teaching become operative in the lives of Christians by means of the activity of the Holy Spirit. Throughout the New Testament the Christian life is presented as being dependent for both its inauguration and its continuance on God's Spirit, who in his ministry confronts men and women with the living Christ, brings them into personal fellowship with God through Christ, and sustains them in all aspects of their new life in Christ. Thus, Christians are said to live their lives 'in the new way of the Spirit, and not in the old way of the written code' (Rom. 7:6), and Christian ministry is portrayed as being 'not of the letter but of the Spirit (2 Cor. 3:6). This is the realization that caused Paul to speak of the Christian as a 'spiritual man' (1 Cor. 2:15; 3:1) and of the Christian life as a 'fellowship with the Spirit' (Phil. 2:1) as well as a 'fellowship with his Son Jesus Christ' (1 Cor. 1:9)."

205. Sweet, VLOG episode 7, *Preach the Story* video.

206. Kennedy, "Remarks at the Dedication of the Aerospace Medical Health Center, San Antonio, Texas, November 21, 1963."

207. Knopp and Castelein, eds., *Taking Every Thought Captive*.

208. Overdorf, *Applying the Sermon*, 50.

209. King, *On Writing*, 174.

210. Overdoff calls this mistake "normalizing." As an example, he cites how Paul chose to circumcise Timothy (Acts 16:1–5) but refused to have Titus circumcised (Gal 2:1–5). Overdorf, *Applying the Sermon*, 92.

211. Robinson, "The Heresy of Application," 20–27.

212. Westpahl, "The Philosophical/Theological Response," 163.

213. Vanhoozer agrees saying, "Note that 'living the Bible' is not quite the same thing as 'applying the Bible.'" Vanhoozer, "A Drama-of-Redemption Model," 170.

214. Casillas quotes *Matter of Interpretation*, 37–38, 45. Casillas, *Beyond Chapter and Verse*, 223.

215. I have no recollection of where I read this. This is just one of those good quotes a preacher hangs on to!

216. Casillas, *Beyond Chapter and Verse*, 223.

217. Robinson, "The Heresy of Application," 20–27.

218. As cited previously, Vanhoozer speaks of "A Drama-of-Redemption Model."

He also uses the word "theodrama" and in doing so addresses Matthew 22:36–40. He says, "Theodrama is both a theoretical framework for understanding God and a theatrical framework for living the Christian life. The goal of the Christian life—to know and love God and our neighbor as ourselves—is essentially a matter of theodramatic understanding." Vanhoozer, *Pictures at a Theological Exhibition*, 168–76.

CONCLUSION

219. Earthly Mission, "The Best Magic Eye Stereograms Around and How to See Them."

Bibliography

Alvord, Bruce W. "The Question of Application in Preaching: The Sermon on the Mount as a Test Case." *Master's Seminary Journal*, vol. 24, no. 1 (Spring 2013) 136.

Blomberg, Craig L. *1 Corinthians*. The NIV Application Commentary. Grand Rapids, MI: Zondervan, 1994.

———. *Interpreting the Parables*. 2nd ed. Downers Grove, IL: IVP Academic, 2012.

Bruce, F. F., et al. *Hard Sayings of the Bible*. Downers Grove, IL: InterVarsity, 1996.

Burge, Gary M. *The New Testament in Seven Sentences: A Small Introduction to a Vast Topic*. Downers Grove, IL: InterVarsity, 2019.

Carson, D. A. *Exegetical Fallacies*. 2nd ed. Grand Rapids, MI: Baker Academic, 1996.

Casillas, Ken. *Beyond Chapter and Verse: The Theology and Practice of Biblical Application*. Eugene, OR: Wipf & Stock, 2018.

Clark, David K. *To Know and Love God: Method for Theology*. Wheaton, IL: Crossway, 2003.

Clarkson, Kari. "12 Hard Stats that Proof the Power of Images." Search Engine People. https://www.searchenginepeople.com/blog/925-image-stats.html.

Craigie, Peter C. *Psalms 1–50*. Word Biblical Commentary. Waco, TX: Word Books, 1983.

Curry, Jack. "Pujols's Shot Recedes in Lidge's Review Mirror." *The New York Times*, October 23, 2005. https://www.nytimes.com/2005/10/23/sports/baseball/pujolss-shot-recedes-in-lidges-rearview-mirror.html.

DeadSea.com. "Why is the Dead Sea Called the Dead Sea?" https://www.deadsea.com/articles-tips/interesting-facts/why-is-the-dead-sea-called-the-dead-sea/.

Dearman, J. Andrew. "Sodom." In *Harper's Bible Dictionary*, edited by P. J. Achtemeier, 974. San Francisco: Harper & Row, 1985.

Doriani, Daniel M. *Putting the Truth to Work: The Theory and Practice of Biblical Application*. Phillipsburg, NJ: P & R, 2001.

———. "A Redemptive-Historical Model." In *Four Views on Moving Beyond the Bible to Theology*, edited by Stanley N. Gundry and Gary T. Meadors, 75–120. Grand Rapids, MI: Zondervan, 2009.

Duvall, J. Scott and J. Daniel Hays. *Grasping God's Word: A Hands-On Approach to Reading, Interpreting, and Applying the Bible*. 3rd ed. Grand Rapids, IL: Zondervan, 2012.

Earthly Mission. "The Best Magic Eye Stereograms Around and How to See Them." https://earthlymission.com/best-magic-eye-stereograms-3d-viewing-explanation/.

Ewert, David. *How to Understand the Bible*. Scottdale, PA: Herald, 2000.

Fee, Gordon D., and Douglas Stuart. *How to Read the Bible for All Its Worth*. 4th ed. Grand Rapids, MI: Zondervan, 2014.

France, R. T. *Women in the Church's Ministry: A Test-Case for Biblical Hermeneutics*. Eugene, OR: Wipf & Stock, 1995.

Geary, James. *I Is an Other: The Secret Life of Metaphor and How It Shapes the Way We See the World*. New York: HarperCollins, 2011.

Grady, Cheryl L., et al. "Neural Correlates of the Episodic Encoding of Pictures and Words." *PNAS* 95, no. 5 (March 3, 1998) 2703–8.

Grenz, Stanley J. with Denise Muir Kjesbo. *Women in the Church: A Biblical Theology of Women in Ministry*. Downers Grove, IL: InterVarsity, 1995.

Guinness World Records. "Best Selling Book." https://www.guinnessworldrecords. com/world-records/best-selling-book-of-non-fiction/.

Kaiser, Walter C., Jr. "A Principlizing Model." In *Four Views on Moving Beyond the Bible to Theology*, edited by Stanley N. Gundry and Gary T. Meadors, 19–50. Grand Rapids, MI: Zondervan, 2009.

———. *Toward an Exegetical Theology: Biblical Exegesis for Preaching and Teaching*. Grand Rapids, MI: Baker, 1981.

Kaiser, Walter C., Jr., et al. *Hard Sayings of the Bible*. Downers Grove, IL: InterVarsity, 1996.

Kaiser, Walter C., Jr., et al., eds. *NIV Archaeological Study Bible*. Grand Rapids, MI: Zondervan, 2005.

Keener, Craig S. *A Commentary on the Gospel of Matthew*. Grand Rapids, MI: Eerdmans, 1999.

———. "An Egalitarian View." In *Two Views on Women in Ministry*, edited by James R. Beck and Craig L. Blomberg, 25–73. Grand Rapids, MI: Zondervan, 2001.

———. *The IVP Bible Background Commentary: New Testament*. 2nd ed. Downers Grove, IL: InterVarsity, 2014.

Kennedy, John F. "Remarks at the Dedication of the Aerospace Medical Health Center, San Antonio, Texas, November 21, 1963." https://www.jfklibrary.org/archives/ other-resources/john-f-kennedy-speeches/san-antonio-tx-19631121.

Kidner, Derek. *Genesis: An Introduction and Commentary*, Vol. 1. Downers Grove, IL: InterVarsity, 1967.

King, Stephen. *On Writing: A Memoir of the Craft*. New York: Simon & Schuster, 2000.

Klein, William M., et al. *Introduction to Biblical Interpretation*. Nashville, TN: Nelson, 2004.

Knopp, Richard A. and John D. Castelein, eds. *Taking Every Thought Captive: Essays in Honor of James D. Strauss*. Joplin, MO: College Press, 1997.

Knowing Jesus. "God Bringing Israel Out of Egypt." https://bible.knowingjesus.com/ topics/God-Bringing-Israel-Out-Of-Egypt.

Kuhatschek, Jack. *Applying the Bible*. Grand Rapids, MI: Zondervan, 1990.

Lakoff, George and Mark Johnson. *Metaphors We Live By*. 2nd ed. Chicago: University of Chicago Press, 2003.

Longenecker, Richard N. *New Testament Social Ethics for Today*. Grand Rapids, MI: Eerdmans, 1984.

———. *New Wine into Fresh Wineskins: Contextualizing the Early Christian Confessions*. Peabody, MA: Hendrickson, 1999.

Lowery, Robert A. *Revelation's Rhapsody: Listening to the Lyrics of the Lamb*. Joplin, MO: College Press, 2006.

Marshall, I. Howard. *Beyond the Bible: Moving from Scripture to Theology*. Grand Rapids, MI: Baker Academic, 2004.

———. *The Gospel of Luke*. The New International Greek Testament Commentary. Grand Rapids, MI: Eerdmans, 1978.

McQuilken, Robertson. *Understanding and Applying the Bible*. Chicago: Moody Press, 1992.

Metzger, Bruce M. *A Textual Commentary on the Greek New Testament, Second Edition a Companion Volume to the United Bible Societies' Greek New Testament*. 2nd ed. New York: United Bible Societies, 1994.

Muller, Richard A. *The Study of Theology: From Biblical Interpretation to Contemporary Formulation*. Grand Rapids, MI: Zondervan, 1991.

Osborne, Grant. *The Hermeneutical Spiral: A Comprehensive Introduction to Biblical Interpretation*. 2nd ed. Downers Grove, IL: InterVarsity, 2006.

Overdorf, Daniel. *Applying the Sermon: How to Balance Biblical Integrity and Cultural Relevance*. Grand Rapids, MI: Kregel, 2009.

Parsons, Noah. "Do Visuals Really Trump Text?" https://www.liveplan.com/blog/scientific-reasons-why-you-should-present-your-data-visually/.

Porter, Stanley E. "Hermeneutics, Biblical Interpretation, and Theology: Hunch, Holy Spirit, or Hard Work?" In *Beyond the Bible: Moving from Scripture to Theology*, edited by I. Howard Marshall, 97–127. Grand Rapids, MI: Baker Academic, 2004.

Richards, Randolph E., and Brandon J. O'Brien. *Misreading Scripture with Western Eyes: Removing Cultural Blinders to Better Understand the Bible*. Downers Grove, IL: InterVarsity, 2012.

Robinson, Haddon W., and Craig Brian Larson, eds., *The Art and Craft of Biblical Preaching*. Grand Rapids, MI: Zondervan, 2005.

Robinson, Haddon W. "The Heresy of Application." *Leadership Journal* 18 (Fall 1997) 20–27.

Schuter, Michael and Roy Clements, *Toward Rediscovering the Old Testament*. Grand Rapids, MI: Zondervan, 1987.

Staton, Knofel. *The Biblical Liberation of Women for Leadership in the Church: As One Essential for the Spiritual Formation of the Church*. Eugene, OR: Wipf & Stock, 2002.

Stein, Robert H. *A Basic Guide to Interpreting the Bible: Playing by the Rules*. Grand Rapids, MI: Baker Academic, 1997.

———. *The Method and Message of Jesus' Teachings*. Louisville, KY: Westminster John Knox Press, 1994.

Sweet, Leonard. "VLOG episode 7." *Preach the Story*. April 2020. https://preachthestory.com/vlog-episode-7/.

Todd, Douglas. "Who Was Canadian Behind Iconic Image of 'Laughing Jesus?'" *Vancouver Sun*, January 13, 2014. https://vancouversun.com/news/staff-blogs/who-created-iconic-image-of-laughing-jesus/.

Vanhoozer, Kevin J. "A Drama-of-Redemption Model." In *Four Views on Moving Beyond the Bible to Theology*, edited by Stanley N. Gundry and Gary T. Meadors, 151–99. Grand Rapids, MI: Zondervan, 2009.

———. "Into the Great Beyond: A Theologian's Response to the Marshall Plan." In *Beyond the Bible: Moving from Scripture to Theology*, I. Howard Marshall, 81–96. Grand Rapids, MI: Baker Academic, 2004.

———. *Pictures at a Theological Exhibition: Scenes of the Church's Worship, Witness and Wisdom*. Downers Grove, IL: IVP Academic, 2016.

Veerman, Dave. *How to Apply the Bible: Discover the Truths of Scripture and Put Them into Practice*. Grand Rapids, MI: Baker, 1993.

Virkler, Henry A. *Hermeneutics: Principles and Processes of Biblical Interpretation*. Grand Rapids, MI: Baker Academic, 2007.

The Visual Bible: Matthew. DVD. Directed by Regardt van den Bergh. South Africa: Visual Bible International, 1993.

Webb, William J. "A Redemptive-Movement Model." In *Four Views on Moving Beyond the Bible to Theology*, edited by Stanley N. Gundry and Gary T. Meadors, 215–48. Grand Rapids, MI: Zondervan, 2009.

———. *Slaves, Women & Homosexuals: Exploring the Hermeneutics of Cultural Analysis*. Downers Grove, IL: InterVarsity, 2001.

Westphal, Merold. "The Philosophical/Theological Response." In *Biblical Hermeneutics: Five Views*, edited by Stanley E. Porter and Beth M. Stovell, 160–73. Downers Grove, IL: IVP Academic, 2012.

Wikipedia. "Johannes Gutenberg." https://en.wikipedia.org/wiki/Johannes_Gutenberg.

Wilmes, Barbara, et al. "Coming to Our Senses: Incorporating Brain Research Findings into Classroom Discussion." *Education* 124, no. 4 (Summer 2008) 659–66.

Wilson, Marvin R. *Our Father Abraham: Jewish Roots of the Christian Faith*. Grand Rapids, MI: Eerdmans, 1989.

Witherington, Ben, III. *Women in the Earliest Churches*. Cambridge: Cambridge University Press, 1988.

Womble, T. Scott. *Beyond Reasonable Doubt: 95 Theses Which Dispute the Church's Conviction Against Women*. USA: Xulon, 2008.

Wright, N. T. *The Last Word: Scripture and the Authority of God—Getting Beyond the Bible Wars*. San Francisco: HarperSanFrancisco, 2005.

Scripture Index

OLD TESTAMENT

Genesis

1:14	x
1:16	x
1:26–27	56
2:18	59
2:20	59
2:24	96
3:13	60
14:1–3	36
14:3	36
14:10	36
16:8	60
18:9	60
19	36, 40
19:1–11	32–33, 36
19:12–29	36–37
21:12	59
22:1–19	17
23:1–2	59
24:10–27	60
37	110

Exodus

15:20	59
20	95
20:8–11	95
38:8	60

Numbers

6:2	60
12:2	59
35:30	95

Deuteronomy

5:12–15	95
6:16	95
12:12	60
12:18	60
17:6	95
19:15	95
22:13–21	30
24:1–5	29
24:1	96
32:11	60

Joshua

10:12–13	118

Judges

4:4	59
4:6–7	59
4:23	59
4:24–27	59
13	59
13:3	60

1 Samuel

1:7	60
13:14	70
21:1–6	95
25:32–33	59

2 Samuel

11:1–12:15	26
20:16	59

2 Kings

19:35	32
22:14	59

Nehemiah

6:14	60

Esther

4:16	59

Psalms

10:1	42
12:2	42
22	68
22:1–2	67–68
22:10	68
22:19	68
51	37
51:1–13	5
51:1–4	26–27
68:11	60
79	67
91:11–12	95
144	67
144:1–2	66

Proverbs

5:15–19	8
6:4	42
21:9	8
22:6	69
26:4–5	71
31:10–31	60

Song of Solomon

4	9
4:10–15	8

Isaiah

8:3	60
40:8	91
40:9	60
41:27	60
55:11	91
64:8	20

Ezekiel

13	60

NEW TESTAMENT

Matthew

2	31
3:8	101
4:1–11	95
4:5–7	107
5–7	5, 18, 94
5	94
5:3–5	18
5:14–16	18
5:17	107
5:21–26	95–96
5:27–30	95
5:29a	74
5:30a	74
5:31–32	95
5:33–37	95
5:38–42	95
5:43–47	95
5:43	41
6:19–21	18, 34
6:22–23	34
6:24	34
6:24b	74
6:28	11
7:1–3	18
7:3–5	71
7:13–14	18
7:24–27	18

8:18–22	73	12:39–40	115
9:17	97	13:34	57
12:1–8	95, 107	15:8–10	18, 57
12:9–14	95	15:11–32	16, 18
12:46–50	95	16:19–31	18
13:44–46	115	17:5	ix
13:51–52	97–98	24:9	57
18:9a	41		
18:15–20	35, 95	**John**	
18:18	35		
19:3–10	29	4:24	60
19:3–9	96	4:29	57
19:3	30	4:39	57
19:16–22	73	8:31–36	102
19:23–26	73–74	8:31–33	43
19:24	17, 28–29	10:3–5	98
20:1–16	115	10:16	98
22:36–40	112, 124	10:27	98
23:37	57	14:12	98
24:43–44	115	14:16–27	98
26:52–53	32	14:16	99
28:10	57	14:17	99
28:19–20	57	14:18	99
		14:20	99
		14:26	99
Mark		16:5–15	98
		16:7	99
2:22	97	16:8–11	99
4:35–41	10	16:13–15	99
5:1–20	21	16:13	99
14:12–13	32	18:3	32
16:7	57	20:14	57
		21:17	57
Luke		21:25	2
1:6	57	**Acts**	
1:28	57		
1:41	57	1–2	98
4	102–03	1:14	57
4:16–21	56	1:26	77
4:18	102	2	75–76
5:19	7	2:1–4	57
5:37–38	97	2:4	77
8:1–3	57	2:17–18	57
8:5–8	18	2:38	77
10:3	13	2:41	75
10:25–37	x	2:42–47	75–76
10:30–37	16, 18	4:31	77
10:38–42	57		

Acts (continued)

5:11	75
5:14	57
5:19	45
6:1–6	78
8:1	75
8:12	58
9–28	45
12:12–17	58
13:1–3	77–78
14:19	6–7, 45
15	121
15:21	121
15:29	90
16	75
16:1–5	123
16:13–15	58
16:15	77
17	75
17:4	58
17:12	58
18	75
18:2	58
19	75
19:10	27
19:23–41	27–28
20:7	77
20:17–38	78
27	45
28:3–5	77

Romans

6:20	102
7:6	123
8:13a	41
16	54
16:1	54
16:3	54
16:6	54
16:7	54
16:12	54
16:15	54
16:16a	41

1 Corinthians

1:9	123

1:11	54
2:10–16	123
2:15	123
3:1	123
11:3–16	55–56
11:5	54
12:1–11	54
12:12–31	55
12:28–31	54
13:12–13	22
14	55
14:1–32	54
14:34–35	46, 54
14:34a	41
14:35	49–50
16:15	54
16:21	7

2 Corinthians

3:1–3	19
3:6	123
10:5	101, 103
11:24–28	37–38
11:25	6
12:7	9

Galatians

2:21b	41
3:26–29	53–54
3:28	53, 86, 109
5:22	101
6:11	7

Ephesians

4:17	41
5	55
5:21	52
5:22–6:9	53
5:22–33	52–53

Philippians

1:7	38
1:13–14	38
1:15	44
1:17	38, 44

1:27	44	2:2	48, 50
1:28	44	2:3	50
2:1	123	2:8-15	47-48
2:2	44	2:8	41, 48
2:14	44	2:9-15	46, 48, 50-51
2:16	13	2:9-10	48, 50
2:21	41	2:9	28
3:2	44	2:10	48
3:18	44	2:11-15	48
4:2-3	53	2:11-12	28
4:2	44	2:11	46
4:4-19	44	2:12	45-61
4:4	37	2:13-15	46
4:10-13	44-45	2:13-14	47
4:13	44-45	2:14-15	28
		2:14	46, 50
		2:15	47, 50, 52

Colossians

		3	52
1:3-8	101	3:1-7	51
1:6	101	3:2-16	50
1:10	101	3:11	28, 46, 50
1:19	64	4:1-5	46, 50
2:2-3	21	4:3-7	50
2:8	102	4:3	28
2:14	9	4:7	28, 46, 50
3:18-4:1	53	4:9-11	50
3:18-19	53	4:12	50
3:22a	41	4:15	50
4:15	53	5:3-16	50
4:18	7	5:3	41
		5:4-10	50

1 Thessalonians

		5:6	28
5:2-10	20	5:9	41
		5:11	28
		5:13-15	28, 46, 52

2 Thessalonians

		5:13	47
3:17	7	5:14	47
		5:25	50
		6:1-2	46, 50

1 Timothy

		6:3-5	46, 50
1:1	50	6:12	50
1:3-4	46, 50	6:20	46, 50
1:6-8	46, 50		
1:16	50-51		
1:19	9	**2 Timothy**	
2:1-3:16	49-50	1:11	51
2:1-7	47	1:13	51
2:1-4	48	2:2	51

2 Timothy (continued)

2:14–3:9	51
2:14	51
2:15	51
2:16–17	51
2:18	51
2:19–22	51
2:23–24	51
2:25	51
2:26	102
3:1	51
3:6–7	51
3:6	28, 46–47, 50
3:7–8	51
4:4	51

Titus

1:5–9	51
1:5–6	52
1:10–11	51
2:1–9	52
2:1	51
2:3–5	51–52
2:7–8	52
2:9	52
2:12	52
2:14	52
3:1–2	52
3:8	52
3:14	52

Philemon

16	54
17	54
19	7

Hebrews

4:12	91
5:12–14	9
11:11	58–59
11:31	58–59
11:32–33	59

James

2:25	58–59

1 Peter

1:15	58
1:17	58
2:5	58
2:9	58
2:12	58
2:14–15	58
2:20	58
3:1–2	58
3:1	58
3:5	58
3:6	58
3:16	58
3:17	58
4:19	58

2 Peter

3:15–16	55

2 John

13	58

Revelation

1:1–6	118
1:4	36
1:6	58
2–3	36
2:7	22
2:9	ix, 22
3:12	22
3:14–22	36
3:22–24	22
5:10	58
12:3	9
13:1–18	30
14:9–11	30
19:19–20	30
20:6	58

CPSIA information can be obtained
at www.ICGtesting.com
Printed in the USA
LVHW021746040921
696733LV00004B/14